A
Trail Runner's
Guide
to
North Wales

By
Jim & Julia
Kelly

TRAIL GUIDES
p u b l i c a t i o n s

First published in Great Britain in 2011 by Trailguides Limited.
www.trailguides.co.uk

ISBN 978-1-905444-50-2

The route diagrams in this book are based upon 1925-1940 Ordnance Survey One Inch maps updated by field trips and site visits.

Trailguides Limited
35 Carmel Road South
Darlington
Co Durham DL3 8DQ

Cover design by Steve Gustard

Printed in Great Britain by the MPG Books Group, Bodmin and King's Lynn.

CONTENTS

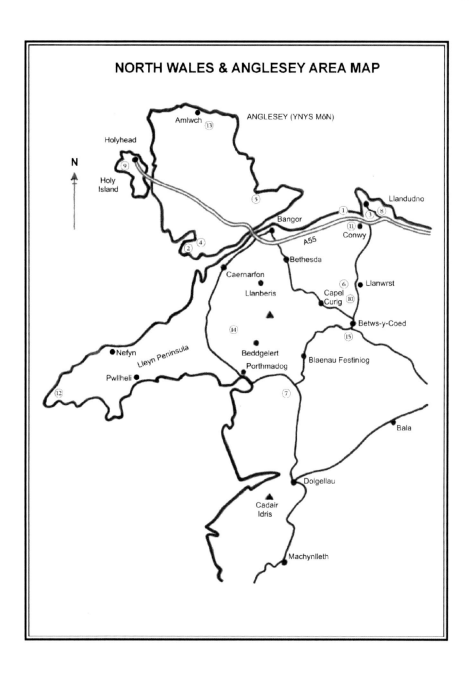

NORTH WALES & ANGLESEY AREA MAP

N

ANGLESEY (YNYS MôN)

Amlwch ⑬

Holyhead

⑨

Holy Island

⑤

Llandudno

Bangor

① ③ ⑧

⑪

Conwy

A55

② ④

Bethesda

Caernarfon

⑥ Llanwrst

Llanberis

Capel Curig ⑩

Betws-y-Coed

⑭

⑮

Nefyn

Lleyn Peninsula

Beddgelert

Blaenau Festiniog

Porthmadog

Pwllheli

⑫

⑦

Bala

Dolgellau

Cadair Idris

Machynlleth

4

ACKNOWLEDGEMENTS

This is now the second Trailguides edition to running in North Wales. Aimed predominantly at the beginner, this all new 'trail runners' guide is owed largely to the dedicated efforts of a long list of valued friends and helpers who persuaded me to compile it. In particular I would like to thank the following:

Zac Laraman of 'Snowdonia Sports Medicine' in Llanberis. Zac provided huge amounts of encouragement with the previous 'Mountain Runner's Guide to Snowdonia' (Trailguides Publishing 2010). It was his idea to produce a follow-up edition aimed at 'rookie' runners wanting to sample trail and off-road running for the very first time or, with limited experience. His section on 'Injury Avoidance for Beginners' is particularly useful and, indeed, essential for anyone venturing onto rough ground for the first time.

Martin Cortvriend, Chairman of the Welsh Fell Running Association who jumped at the chance to write the 'Foreword' to this guide. Martin has a very keen interest in trail running in North Wales and sees this as a huge area of development over the next few years.

Also, members of the Eryri Committee who supported and encouraged me during the guides' production.

Above all, I would like to thank my wife, Julia for yet more hours of hard work either sat in-front of the laptop night after night, producing text and graphics or, stood alongside paths and woodland trails, snapping pictures of me running past! Amazingly, this time round, Julia has even taken to jogging some of these delightful routes herself! Her contribution to this guide has been enormous.

Final thanks go to Keven Shevels and Trailguides Publishing Ltd., for his continued commercial support and belief in my efforts to produce high quality running guides to this beautiful area of the United Kingdom.

Jim Kelly.

TRAIL RUNNING: A definition

Trail running is a variant on running that differs from tarmac road and artificial track running. Trail running generally takes place on hiking trails, most commonly single track trails and gravel roads. Trails tend to traverse varying terrain; hills, mountains, forests and coastlines. The British Athletics Federation state that trail running uses footpaths and bridleways marked on OS Maps as "public rights of way." They are 'highways' to which pedestrians have unrestricted access under English law. Other forms of track such as tow paths, cart tracks and paths in parks are excluded due to them often requiring the owner's permission in order to run them. Bear in mind that because a track shows on an OS map, it doesn't necessarily mean you have a right to use it.

FOREWORD

Following on from his excellent guide to fell running routes in North Wales, Jim Kelly has excelled himself with another detailed compendium of off-road routes. Fellrunners, by and large, are a strange and hardy breed, finding a masochistic pleasure in galloping up the steepest, roughest climbs to the highest peaks and Jim's previous book has catered for them very well. Trail running and trail walking, on the other hand, appeals to a wider audience and would be a faster growing phenomenon if only people knew where to go. The answer is in your hands! Discovering appropriate and suitable trail routes is not always straightforward but, for the first time, an easy to follow but comprehensively detailed guide is available.

Jim Kelly is an avid runner on both mountain and trail and competes regularly in many events in North Wales, usually with a big grin on his face. Based in Northern Snowdonia, he has access to some of the finest countryside that Wales has to offer and has clearly explored the tracks and trails of the North of Wales extensively. What particularly distinguishes Jim's guides is the attention to detail that derives from his first-hand experience of finding his way through changing landscapes. He expertly pinpoints features that aid navigation, but at the same time draws attention to the historical curiosities and varied scenery that make running or walking in North Wales such a pleasure. All this only comes from thorough research and Jim and his wife Julia, have clearly had a whale of a time exploring the routes, assembling the vast amount of information contained in the guide and taking pictures of each other.

I can thoroughly recommend this guide to beginners to trail running and walking, and visitors to North Wales who may not be so familiar with our tracks and trails, but I am sure that it will also find its way onto the bookshelves of more experienced runners and walkers including old timers like myself!

Martin Cortvriend
Chairman
Welsh Fell Runners Association

7

PREFACE

North Wales, has long been the outdoor activity playground for both residents and visitors since way back in Victorian times. Its majestic, rugged mountains, rounded fells and dramatic coastlines have continually drawn interest from rock climbers, mountaineers, walkers, water-sports enthusiasts, cyclists and, of course, not forgetting, the thousands of ordinary, casual tourists that flock to the region year on year.

However, the largest activity "growth area" over the last few years has been the increase in numbers of men and women using the region for fell and trail running. For sure, fell running in Snowdonia has a historic and varied tradition and, indeed, some of the sports' greatest National fell runners established their reputations and records here. Back in the 1970's and 1980's, the likes of Paddy Buckley and Colin Donnelly were posting ground-breaking, personal best times on some of the areas longest challenges. Amazingly, many of these records hold and still remain unbroken, posing a considerable challenge for today's fell running "young guns" and elite runners. Of particular interest are the records established by Kenny Stuart and Robbie Bryson in 1985 during the famous (infamous?!) Snowdon Race. Although Robbie was first to the top in a staggering 39.47 minutes, it was Kenny who pulled away on the descent and posted a record time of 1.02.29. Both records are still intact... 25 years on!! Kenny also still holds the record for the Ben Nevis Race in the Scottish Highlands in the same year in a time of 01.25.34 ; A truly staggering achievement!

So, why is off-road running becoming so popular? Well, apart from the obvious health-related benefits involved with the sport (see other TRAILGUIDES "Coaching Off-Road Running" Series publications), trail running is also a very "accessible" pastime. It can be practised by almost any reasonably fit person with basic equipment a fraction of the cost of some other outdoor sports. Add to this a fantastic, diverse, scenic landscape, with stunning, challenging routes for all levels of ability, and one is left with what is perhaps the one of the most rewarding, enjoyable "running cocktails" to be consumed anywhere in the UK.

It was for these reasons I felt compelled to create the previous, very successful guide, "A Mountain Runner's Guide to Snowdonia". This all-new Trail Runner's Guide to North Wales is aimed primarily at the novice runner who wants to make the transition from the treadmill or urban tarmac to the great off-road outdoors. Whether you are a resident of North Wales or an "out of county" visitor, this book will provide the trail runner with not only experienced, first-hand advice but also, detailed, accurate route descriptions, safety and environmental considerations and a wealth of other, invaluable local information that will serve to assist and enhance any runner's experience in this magnificent area. With routes from easy 4 milers to more demanding, lengthy forest and coastal challenges, there is something here to suit everyone and cater for all abilities. And, for the "tickers" and "competitive upstarts" amongst us, there is even a tick-sheet thrown in for good measure!

Jim Kelly, 2011

INTRODUCTION

North Wales, with its Snowdonia National Park, is a strikingly beautiful area which has a wealth of wildlife, history, legends, culture and heritage. In terms of diversity, it is one of the UK's largest and most natural areas. The fantastic, clean, golden beaches, mixed woodlands and heather covered uplands leading to the high peaks of Snowdon and Cadair Idris attract visitors from all over the British Isles and from abroad. However, the specific group of people we are concerned with here are the hundreds of trail, fell and mountain runners who are either fortunate enough to live in the area or, visit from other parts of the U.K. North Wales, Snowdonia in particular, is often referred to as the "adventure playground" for the populations of the cities of Liverpool and Manchester. Easy, direct motorway access from the north west via the M6, M56 and the superb A55 North Wales Coast Road, means the very heart of Snowdonia can be accessed by car in around two hours for a great many people. In addition to this, the region is also served by a good range of both internal and external public transport (for enquiries go to: www.traveline.org.uk or, call 0871 200 2233).

Over the last few years running, as a sport and fitness activity, has probably seen the biggest growth compared with any other outdoor sport. Everyone has their own set of intrinsic reasons for running. However, the common denominators must be the tremendous aerobic health benefits, its relatively low cost and the simple fact that running can be easily accessed to "fit-in" with a busy modern lifestyle and people's work commitments. The disciplines of trail, fell and mountain running have especially seen a massive surge in participant numbers (and ever increasing sales of fell running kit in the shops…I hasten to add!). One only has to look at the large race numbers for most club-organised fell running events each week across Britain, to confirm this. It is also true to say that many UK running clubs now actively arrange weekend visits to "other hilly or remote areas" for their members. The same can be said for the many individuals who also visit. That said, participants in other outdoor sports such as, rock climbing, walking and caving have always done this so there's nothing unusual in that department! The big questions are; Where do you run? Where do you stay? And, which routes should you do? Normal practice is generally to purchase a guide/ route book and plan your days accordingly. Unfortunately, for trail and mountain runners, definitive "area or *route* guides" are few and far between. That is,…until now! For sure, you are always going to find the odd club that may produce its own local guidebook/ route card but, these are not necessarily widely available to the masses through regional or national running shops. The aim of this guide is to provide the runner, whether local or visitor, with detailed, valuable, first-hand route information on fifteen of North Wales' best trail runs. More significant is the fact that this is the first ever complete North Wales trail running route guide aimed primarily at novice runners. It even has a "tick list" at the back aimed at those who are seduced by the 'ceremonial ticking/ high-lighter pen ritual' in the pub or café afterwards!

For consistency with other Trailguides in the series, the Ferguson Grading System ('FGS') has been adopted as a means of assessing the nature and severity of the various trail runs in this book and the abilities and equipment needed to tackle each one safely. Developed by Stuart Ferguson, a long time fell and trail runner and general outdoor enthusiast, the FGS is the most accurate and comprehensive grading system to compare off-road trail and mountain running anywhere in the country.

FERGUSON GRADING SYSTEM:

Tables 1& 2, set out on the next two pages, are used in order to give a grading to each run. Table 1 sets out three categories of country that a route could potentially cross, together with a range of factors that would need to be considered when tackling that route. The three categories are: Trail, Fell and Mountain, and after assessing which category best fits the route, a letter 'T','F' or 'M', is allocated to that route. Where a route does not fit perfectly into one of the three categories the closest category is allocated.

Table 2 deals with five specific aspects of the route namely distance, navigation, terrain, remoteness and height gain, and each one is allocated a letter 'D','N','T','R' or 'H'. Each letter is also given a severity score from the range 0-3 or 0-4, in respect of distance ('D'). The higher the number, the more severe the run. The five severity scores are then added together to give an overall score. The overall score is then put with the Table 1 category letter (i.e. 'T','F' or 'M').

In order to show how the grading has been determined for each run in this guide, the five individual severity scores are set out, in square brackets, immediately after the actual grading. So, for example, Route 1 has a grading of T3 [D1, N1,T0,R1,H0], indicating that it is a Trail Category run with a total severity score of 3. This is made up of the five specific severity scores, for distance ('D'), navigation ('N'), terrain ('T'), remoteness ('R') and height gain ('H'), of

TABLE 1

	TRAIL	FELL	MOUNTAIN
Description	Lowland and forest areas including urban, cultivated and forested locations.	Moorlands and upland areas which may include some upland cultivated and forestry areas plus possibly remote locations.	Upland and mountain areas including remote and isolated locations.
Height	Not usually above 1,000 feet but may go up to 2,500 feet	Usually above 1,000 feet, up to 2,500 feet and above.	Usually above 2,500 feet and up to 4,000 feet.
Way-marking	Usually	Limited	None
Terrain	Usually graded paths, tracks and trails but may include some off-trail	May include some graded paths, tracks and trails but mainly off-trail	Virtually all off-trail
Height gain	Limited height gain	May include considerable height gain	May include some severe height gain.
Effects of weather	Very limited effect	May be prone to sudden weather changes	Extreme weather a possibility
Navigational skills	None to basic	Basic to competent	Competent to expert
Equipment	Running - Trail shoes Possibly waterproofs Food and drink dependant upon route	Running - Trail/fell shoes Full waterproof cover. Possibly map and compass dependant upon route. Food and drink dependant upon route	Running - Fell shoes Full waterproof cover Map and compass Food and drink
Escape Routes	Yes	Some	Some to nil

TABLE 2

Score	0	1	2	3	4
Distance	Up to 6 miles	6 – 12 miles	12 – 18 miles	18 miles +	24 miles +
Navigation	No navigation skills needed	Basic navigation skills needed	Competent navigation skills needed	Expert navigation skills needed	
Terrain	75% + on graded track or path	50 – 75% on graded track or path 25 – 50% off track	25 -50% on graded track or path 50 – 75% off track	Under 25% on graded track or path Over 75% off track	
Remoteness	Urban	Countryside in fairly close proximity to habitation – at least 80% of the route within 2 miles	Countryside not in close proximity to habitation – less than 20% of the route within 2 miles	Remote, isolated location	
Height gain	Less than 100 ft per mile	Over 100 ft per mile	Over 125 ft per mile	Over 250 ft per mile	

Notes to Table 2

Graded paths = Well established paths with a stable surface.
Escape routes = The opportunity to cut the route short and return to the start without completing the full course in the event of weather changes or unforeseen incidents.

1,1, 0,1 and 1 respectively. The highest total severity score which can be achieved is 16 and the lowest total severity score achievable is 0.

The table which accompanies the grading at the start of each running route sets out the specific factors, extracted from Table 2, that need to be considered when tackling that particular run.

MAPS:

Three maps are required to cover the full area of Snowdonia National Park; Ordnance Survey 1:25,000 Explorer Maps OL17 which covers the northern section, OL18 the central and OL23 the southern section. In addition to these, Outdoor Leisure Sheets 262 and 263 of the Isle of Anglesey would be useful. The relevant map will be shown in the details of the individual run. The hand drawn maps reproduced in this guide act as route diagrams only and do not necessarily contain the vital relief and other detailed information that the Ordnance Survey maps provide. Whilst under normal conditions they should be sufficient to guide you round the run they are not intended to replace the use of the relevant map. The terrain of North Wales and Snowdonia is generally wild and rough, which is largely its attraction. As a result, the local weather patterns can be very unpredictable. It is quite possible to set off in brilliant sunshine and then to find that later, low cloud, mist and rain has come rolling in and with marked reductions in visibility. So, although some of these routes can be tackled with a minimum of navigational skill, the ability to navigate with map and compass is a 'preferred' skill to run safely along these trails and coastlines. If you intend to purchase any or, all, of these maps may I also suggest that you opt for the laminated version(s). Although more expensive in the first place, they are fully waterproof and will stand up to the rigors of being put in and out of hydration belts and packs far more than their ordinary paper counterparts. A non-laminated map in regular use in any outdoor environment will last no time! Money wasted.

WEATHER:

As already mentioned, the weather in North Wales can be very changeable even during the summer months. The exposed altitude of some of the high mountains can make even a balmy summer's day seem cold and uninviting. When you are near the top of one of these high summits or plateaus, mist, wind and rain can be experienced no matter the time of year and this can change quite quickly catching the trail or fell runner unaware. Indeed, many of the higher peaks, particularly in the Snowdon Group, can generate their own mini-weather systems. It is quite possible for the tops and rocky ridges to be shrouded in mist and drizzle while the surrounding valleys and coastal lowlands are bathed in glorious sunshine! The message is, don't underestimate this high country!! Recent winters in Snowdonia have been quite harsh with snow lying on the highest peaks from as early as October through to early April!. Whether these climatic trends continue remains to be seen. Basically, no matter the time of year, when running in this region, be prepared and equipped for all weather conditions. Expect the unexpected.

EQUIPMENT:

This one is always tricky. What to wear? What not to wear? What to take with you? What to leave behind? What if I need this? What if I don't? As I have discovered during many training runs and events, it is very difficult to get it right every time. If you are new to the sport of trail running may I suggest you also purchase a copy of "An Introduction to Trail and Fell Running" (Trailguides ISBN 1-905444-12-5) to accompany this area guide. There is a very good chapter on kit choice and mountain safety, especially if you are training alone! You will find, with experience and common sense, your ability to judge what you are likely to need will improve over time. A basic rule of thumb is, there is no point in packing enough kit to traverse the Gobi Desert if your run is less than five or six miles across the lowlands in warm spring sunshine! However, if your journey is 12 miles plus, across high country in remote, unfamiliar mountains and likely to take 3 hours or more, with uncertain weather conditions, then it's a different story! Most importantly, travel light. Opt for wearing non-cotton based fabrics that resist moisture retention and wick away sweat. In spring and summer a lightweight vest, shorts and cap is fine. Also consider whether you may need sunbloc! However, in winter, a short or long-sleeved compression top, lightweight waterproof shell top and compression running tights "combo" might sound more sensible. It's a personal choice regarding whether to use either a hydration back-pack or waist belt, "bum-bag". Whichever one you feel more comfortable with, essential kit in both should include map (and this Trailguide?!), compass, whistle, watch/GARMIN G.P.S., silver survival bag, energy drink/gel, mobile phone(*), running hat/cap, gloves, "Buff" (optional) and wind/waterproof shell top/ bottoms. The most Important thing is to be comfortable. Also, make sure that you pack a clean set of clothes and footwear in the car to get changed into afterwards. There's nothing worse than driving back to wherever(?) covered in mud, with soaking wet feet, wearing sweaty running kit, in a desperate battle to prevent the car windows from steaming up! Yep, we've all done it! Not pleasant. If you notice, choice of footwear has been omitted. In the past, fell and mountain running was dominated by Walsh Shoes. However, in the last few years, the choice has widened enormously with the likes of Montrail, Saloman and INOV8 producing specialist shoes for different terrain, events and foot-type. The advice is, if in doubt, seek specialist help from your running shop, club or magazine reviews. (*) Please note that although mobile network coverage across the UK is more or less complete – depending on your provider of course! However, please remember that signal strength in mountainous or hilly areas is unpredictable. Whilst it can be full strength on the summits, back down in the sheltered valleys, surrounded by cliffs, it often fluctuates between one or two bars or, at worse, no signal whatsoever. The advice is; by all means take a mobile but be mindful that it could fail when you need it most! (see section on Mountain Safety/ Emergency Procedures)

INJURY AVOIDANCE

In association with

ZacLaraman
Snowdonia Sports Medicine

If you're reading this you're either about to buy this guide or already have! And you've decided that you fancy giving trail running a go. So what's so great about trail running compared to road running…..?

Well from my perspective as a sports injury professional it's a great way, if done properly, for you to stay out of my clinic and out of the GP's surgery, and that's all we really want…a healthier, fitter population. So how do you avoid the pain, inconvenience, and financial outlay of trail running injuries? My advice would be to spend a little money now to avoid paying a lot more in the future and avoid all the pain and inconvenience of an overuse injury.

**Zac Laraman,
BSc (Hons) Osteopathy,
GOsC**

16

Find a recommended Sports Osteopath, Sports Physiotherapist or Sports Physician and get a full musculoskeletal and biomechanical assessment first. This may show up any weaknesses or problems that are individual to you. These professionals should then give you advice on foot biomechanics, flexibility and conditioning outside of running.

Because running on roads is repetitive; the terrain seldom alters; the force that your body generates against gravity is not dissipated as well on tarmac as it is on softer ground so the impact is higher per foot fall when road running than it might be on a trail run.

Running on trails requires greater concentration than on road because, in simple terms, there are more obstacles in your path than on the road. So, trail running requires an active sense of awareness and therefore keeps the mind active and improves reflexes. The constant change in terrain with each foot fall also trains your body's balance, your proprioceptors become more responsive and your overall muscular strength improves.

Like with any activity, too much of the same exercise can start to create and exacerbate muscular imbalances which may lead to further problems in the future.

You may also need to re-evaluate your equipment. Trail shoes are a snugger fit so that your feet can 'feel' and respond to the terrain quicker and so avoid ankle sprains and the like. Your therapist will be able to recommend the correct footwear for you particular foot type;

Incorrect trainer fit can have a knock on effect throughout the body as illustrated in the diagram...they can send your entire body off kilter and see you back in my clinic for some extensive rehabilitation!

However lovely the scenery is....you're still outdoors in a climatically hostile environment, so be prepared for changes in weather...lightweight waterproofs, plenty of water, perhaps a water-bladder carried in a small pack on your back where you can keep a map, food, camera and perhaps a torch just in case, when trail running although it is a fantastic alternative to road running...you are out in the wild so take extra precautions and perhaps initially run with a group or partner.

Zac Laraman

MOUNTAIN SAFETY AND EMERGENCY PROCEDURES:

Safety has got to be on the mind of every runner whether you are just running round the block or running on the trails in and around the mountains of North Wales. The safety of yourself and anybody that you are running with, first of all rests with you! Even on a relatively "safe" low level route accidents and injuries can and do happen. If you are running alone, always tell someone where you are going and when you expect to be back. However, don't forget to tell them that you **are** back. Otherwise, you run the risk of causing, what Mountain Rescue define as, a "false call with good intent!"

If a serious accident does occur that requires you to be immobile then stop and try to find some shelter. If you are carrying a survival bag/space blanket use it. Ensure that you maintain your body temperature. Having stopped running you will quickly get chilled and cold. Use your whistle or mobile phone to summon help. The International Distress Call is six strong blasts of the whistle followed by a minutes silence, then repeat as necessary. Also, remember the point already mentioned regarding mobile phone signal limitations. However, if your phone has signal, **dial 999 and ask for North Wales Police, Mountain Safety.** If you manage to get through, the **MRT** (Mountain Rescue Team) will require essential factual information such as your exact location, grid reference (if possible), person(s) involved and extent of the injury.

In the event of a helicopter evacuation, **ALL** runners or persons in the immediate area should take heed; A helicopter flying close to rocks or ridges will make verbal communication between anyone on the ground almost impossible. Be wary of any loose debris being blown around by the rotor downdraft. An orange smoke grenade may be dropped from the helicopter to give wind direction. Assistance should only be given to the helicopter crew/personnel if requested. A helicopter will always be flown into the wind to effect a rescue and, on landing, there are three danger points; the main rotor, the tail rotor and the engine exhaust. The helicopter should not be approached until directed to do so by the air crew.

Remember, you can reduce the risk to yourself and others by ensuring that you plan and time your runs effectively, carry and wear the correct equipment, possess adequate navigational knowledge/skills and pay attention to local weather conditions. If in doubt, be prepared to adapt/modify your run accordingly. Occasionally, it is wise to allow discretion to be the better part of running valour!

TRAIL RUNNING: A definition

Trail running is a variant on running that differs from tarmac road and artificial track running. Trail running generally takes place on hiking trails, most commonly single track trails and gravel roads. Trails tend to traverse varying terrain; hills, mountains, forests and coastlines. The British Athletics Federation state that trail running uses footpaths and bridleways marked on OS Maps as "public rights of way." They are 'highways' to which pedestrians have unrestricted access under English law. Other forms of track such as tow paths, cart tracks and paths in parks are excluded due to them often requiring the owner's permission in order to run them. Bear in mind that because a track shows on an OS map, it doesn't necessarily mean you have a right to use it.

WHERE TO STAY:

Like in any of the UK's National Park designated areas, the list of places to stay in Snowdonia is probably about as long as the rail tracks extending from Llanberis to Snowdon summit! However, as a starting point, I have listed several establishments that offer a warm welcome and reasonable rates for an overnight stay or two.

Camping/ Bunkhouse Accommodation:

Eric's Café, Campsite & Bunkhouse, Bwlch y Moch, Tremadog, Gwynedd LL49 9SN. Owned by Eric Jones, the legendary climber, mountaineer, freefall parachutist and 'original' adrenaline junkie! Amazingly, he's still doing it all and he's in his seventies! Great location for southern/ central Snowdonia runs. Tel: 01766 512199/ 0777 1482321 for bookings. Email: climbtremadog@aol.com

Pete's Eats, 40 High Street, Llanberis, LL55 4EU. Bunkhouse/ dormitory accommodation. Tel: 01286 870117. Website: www.petes-eats.co.uk
Pentre Bach (Bach Ventures Ltd.) Campsite & Bunkhouse, Waunfawr, Nr. Caernarfon LL54 7AG. Nice campsite, great location, barn sleeps up to 16 persons. Tel: 01286 650643.

The Eagles ,Penmachno.
Conwy, LL24 0UG. Owned by Linda & Gerry McMorrow, Tel: 01690 760177
Half an hour to all of Wales' 3000ft Peaks. Half a mile to the Penmachno bike and trail route.

20

Conwy, Lledr, Llugwy & Ogwen only a short drive. Central to most areas.
Email: inn@eaglespenmachno..co.uk
Website : www.eaglespenmachno.co.uk

Hotels/ Bed & Breakfast:

The Tilstone , 15, Carmen Sylva
Road, Llandudno, LL30 1EQ
Tel: 01492 8755888
Website : www.tilstonehotel.co.uk .
The Tilstone is owned and run by
Lynne & Steve Jones, offering
personal touch of a family run
business. Ideal location for trail
running along the North Wales Coast.

Run to the Hills (North Wales) B&B,
4 Esplanade, Penmaenmawr,Gwynedd
LL34 6LU. Tel. 01492 622662.
Email :james_julia.kelly@yahoo.co.uk
http://runtothehills.bardbank.co.uk
B&B accommodation for up to 3
persons. Owned by Jim & Julia Kelly,
and offered as part of their guided
running courses. However can be
booked on an 'accommodation'
only basis. Good value for money,
great breakfast & a warm welcome!

Tyddyn Llwyn Caravan & Touring Park, Morfa Bychan Road, Porthmadog,
Gwynedd LL49 9UR. Situated beneath Moel y Gest, this is an ideal location
for runners owning a caravan/camper van. Very sheltered site and the owner,
Peter Wright, is very 'pro-fell running". Tent pitches also available. Tel:
01766 512205. Website: www.tyddynllwyn.com

The Legacy Royal Victoria Hotel, Llanberis LL55 4TY. The 'original' hotel
in Llanberis. Big and 'touristy' but that's part of its charm.
Tel: 0870 832 9903. Website : www.legacy-hotels.co.uk

WHERE TO EAT:

Being the tourist destination it is, North Wales has a massive variety of restaurants, cafes, pubs and takeaways. Like anywhere, some are exceptionally good, some are bad and some are.. well, downright ugly! Depending on your location/ 'base-camp', you may wish to consider any of the following;

Asha Balti House, Denbigh Street, Llanwrst, Nr. Conwy LL26 0LL.
Tel: 01492 641910
Website: www.asha-balti-house.co.uk.
Award winning curry house. Probably the best in North Wales! Excellent menu, service and atmosphere.

Pete's Eats, 38-40 High Street, Llanberis. Pete's is an 'institution' and has been the 'focal-point'/ meeting place for rock climbers, walkers, cyclists etc. for as long as anyone can remember. Offers great food and lots of it at reasonable prices. The menu should satisfy any runner's appetite at the end of a tough day out on the trails. Open 8am – 8pm.

Le Bistro, 23 Hole in the Wall Street, Caernarfon LL55 1RF. Tel. 01286 672131. e-mail lebistro23@aol.com. Owned by Jacky and Linda Boulet. Jacky is a very active fell runner so a warm welcome is guaranteed to anyone producing or mentioning this book when they order! "Tres bon cuisine!"

The Beach Cafe, The Promenade, Penmaenmawr, Conwy, LL34 6AY.
Tel: 01492 623885 . Run by Nicky & Kevin Hughes. A friendly, beach front Cafe serving a traditional menu and a range of light bites and beverages. Also

serves a nice range of homemade cakes. An ideal spot for a relaxing 'brew' after running the Conwy Area Trails and enjoying the clean and gorgeous beach of Penmaenmawr.

Pen y Ceunant Isaf Tea Rooms, Snowdon Path, Llanberis, LL55 4UW. Tel: 01286 872606. Restored 18th C. Cottage café run by Stefan Roberts, en route to Snowdon summit. Log fires, tea, cakes and locally bottled real ales. Fantastic!

RSPB South Stack Visitor Centre, South Stack,Holyhead,Anglesey, LL65 1YH, Ph: 01407 762100 Email: south.stack@rspb.org.uk
Website: www.rspb.org.uk/southstack
Catering manager: Jon Ward ; Site Manager Dave Bateson
In a truly stunning location, South Stack Visitor Centre is open year round from 10am - 5pm. The café serves a range of freshly prepared food using locally sourced ingredients throughout the day with Breakfast 10 – 11, Lunch 11-3; Tea 3 -5. Also available as a venue for private functions and groups during and outside these opening hours by arrangement.

TOURIST INFORMATION CENTRES & WEBSITES:

Within Snowdonia there are... wait for it, 11 (yes, 11!) Tourist Information Centres (TIC's) serving the mountains and coastal regions. There are also 6 "Snowdonia National Park Information Centres". Contact details for the main TIC's are as follows:

Llanberis Tourist Information Centre, 41A High Street, Llanberis. Tel: 01286 870765.

Beddgelert Tourist Information Centre, Canolfan Hotel Hebog, Beddgelert. Tel: 01766 890615.

Snowdonia Nat. Park Information Centre (Betws-y-Coed). Tel: 01690 710426.

Snowdonia Nat. Park Information Centre (Blaenau Ffestiniog). Tel: 01766 830360.

Dolgellau Tourist Information Centre, Ty Meirion, Eldon Square, Dolgellau. Tel:01341 422888.

In addition to the TIC's the Snowdonia National Park Authority also operate a very useful website giving information on places to visit, places to eat and shop as well as advice on other leisure activities in the area. The website can be found at: www.eryri-npa.gov.uk

Other websites worth looking are: www.attractionsofsnowdonia.com and www.visitsnowdonia.info

FELL RUNNING WEBSITES:

For specific information relating to Snowdonia/ Welsh fell running, races and results contact:

Rhedwyr ERYRI Harriers Running Club:
www.eryriharriers.org.uk

24

Welsh Fell Runners Association (WFRA): www.wrfa.org.uk

Welsh Athletics (Athletau Cymru) Ltd:
www.welshathletics.org

Run to the Hills, North Wales, Guided off-road running services :
http://runtothehills.bardbank.co.uk

Mud Sweat and Tears, worldwide off-road running
http://www.mudsweatandtears.co.uk

Fabian4 Events
For an interesting selection of Trail and other running
races, including the Sandstone Trail in Cheshire, the
Welsh 1000m Peaks race, and a great 2 day event in
the French Alps (OMM France), check out the
"Triathlon, Running, Mountain Marathons" tab on
www.fabian4.co.uk.

ROUTE 1

Llanfairfechan Coastal Path

ROUTE 1
Llanfairfechan Coastal Path

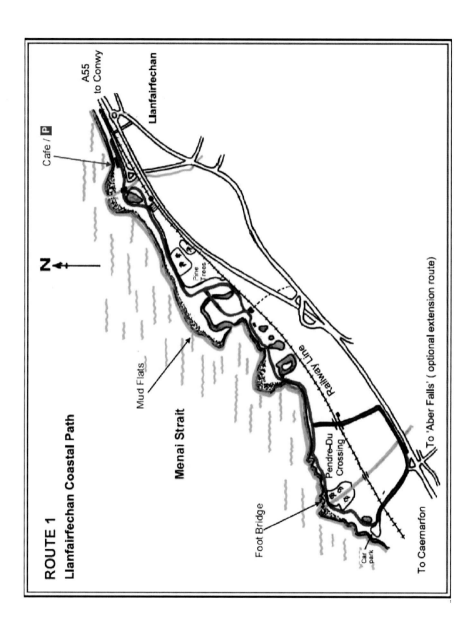

N

Cafe / P

A55
to Conwy

Llanfairfechan

Pine Trees

Mud Flats

Menai Strait

Railway Line

Foot Bridge

Pendre-Du Crossing

To 'Aber Falls' (optional extension route)

Car park

To Caernarfon

ROUTE 1: LLANFAIRFECHAN COASTAL PATH

DISTANCE: 6.5 Miles
ASCENT: Min. 5 metres @ start. Max.20 metres.
TERRAIN: This superb, picturesque route involves some of the best coastal terrain and scenery to be found in this area. This is an ideal route for someone making the transition from tarmac to gentle off-road running. It is a delightful mix of path, track, road and beach surfaces, the majority of which are on the 'flat'. The route does not require specialist trail / fell running shoes. The views across the Menai Strait towards Anglesey and Puffin Island are always in sight.
  Facing Westerly, on a clear spring or summer's evening the sunsets are simply tremendous. There are no tidal restrictions. However, like all coastal runs, it can be prone to very strong winds that tend to 'funnel' through the Menai Strait. Advice is to avoid days like this and seek the shelter of a gentle forest trail run instead!
For the more adventurous and / or energetic, this route can be 'linked' with a continuation into the village of Abergwyngregyn and up to the famous 'Aber Falls' waterfall. This adds a further 4 miles there and back, using the minor road and good tourist track, to the waterfall itself.
TIME: 50 minutes to 1hr. approx. depending on weather etc. *(Allow extra 35 - 45 minutes if extending to Aber Falls and back!)*
START: Llanfairfechan Promenade/ Café car park.
O.S MAP: 1:25,000 Sheet North Wales OL17.
GRADIENT: Flat throughout apart from one gentle road ascent.
ACCESS: The whole area is designated a Wildlife Nature Reserve. It provides a migratory and permanent home for a wide variety of seabirds and other wildlife. It is no surprise to be out running and see the occasional Buzzard hovering above you or hear the gentle cries of oyster catchers out on the mud flats. Please keep to all marked footpaths and obey any seasonal restrictions or requests.

Grid References
680755 Llanfairfechan Café / car park (free)
669747 Right turn over raised track above salt marsh / mudflats.
649736 Footbridge over Afon Aber.
648731 Nature reserve car park
652728 Left turn into minor road before A55 'Aber' junction
657735 Pentre Du unmanned railway crossing. BEWARE HST's!
656738 Right turn back on to coastal path

FGS Grading: Grading is T3 [D1, N1, T0, R1, H0]

Distance	1	6 – 12 miles
Navigation	1	Basic navigation skills needed
Terrain	0	75% on graded track or path
Remoteness	1	Countryside in fairly close proximity to habitation – at least 80% of the route within 2 miles
Height	0	Less than 100 ft per mile

Route Description :

1 Start this run by either parking at the free car park adjacent to the beach front café (**GR 680755**) or, alternatively, a little further up the road overlooked by the large Victorian houses. There are also public conveniences at the free car park, if needed. Proceed through the large metal kissing gate over the stream which gives access to the old boating lake – now populated by ducks and swans. The footpath around this is tarmac and runs along the seafront for half a mile or so, passing through another kissing gate with some fenced off pine woods to your left. The tarmac path continues past this until it reaches the end of the 'promenade' by a metal bench seat.

The Author, Jim Kelly approaching the end of the tarmac section past the pine woods. The beach front of Llanfairfechan and The Great Orme is way back in the distance. Photo by Julia Kelly.

2. From here the path becomes grass as it curves round to the left and then takes a sharp right across an 'elevated' section bisecting the mud/ salt marsh area (**GR 669747**). Continue to run along this as it veers to he left again and up towards a house marked as, "Glan y mor Elias" on the OS Map. A large Nature Reserve information board here explains the significance on the area, in terms of its wildlife diversity.

3. At Glan y mor Elias cross over the small stream and connect with the narrow, sandy path along the top of the beach. Do not take the immediate left turn here as you will end up at one of the wooden bird hides and be forced to back-track! Continue running in front of the bird hide and along the broken coastal path. This is a mix of sand, rocks, cobbles and grassy sections. It is above the high tide boundary so it should be accessible in all but the roughest sea/ wave conditions. In which case, you wouldn't be there running in the first place!

4. This path continues pleasantly for some distance. Eventually, a small, purpose-built, wooden footbridge is met amongst some trees. This allows pedestrians to cross over the Afon Aber (**GR 649736**). Please note that the areas either side of the river can tend to get a bit on the boggy side, especially after heavy rain. After the footbridge a (sometimes) muddy path leads on to a better cart track with a large yellow sign by it warning any 'contractors' that there is a 'pipeline' under the ground at this point!

5. This track leads past another car park (**GR 648731**) serving the second bird hide. Run past the car park, over a cattle grid and on to a narrow, tarmac country lane, leading uphill very gently. This heads up to the village of Abergwyngregyn and the famous 'Aber Falls' waterfall at the top of the valley (see note re. optional extension from this point!).

6. Before the Aber/ A55 junction, take the left turn continuation of this country lane (**GR 652728**), wide at first and then becoming narrow after a sharp left bend (grass growing in he middle of the road at this point!).

Run pleasantly down this until you reach the un-manned railway crossing of 'Pentre Du' and a house on the right (**GR 657735**). *PLEASE TAKE GREAT CARE! THE HIGH SPEED TRAIN (HST) FROM ANGLESEY TO CHESTER RUNS THROUGH HERE.* Obey the instructions and cross as quickly as possible. Once over the other side, continue running down the narrow grassy track, bordered on both sides by hedgerow. After a little way, this emerges once again on the narrow, broken coastal path (**GR 656738**). Turn right here and retrace your running steps back to Glan y mor Elias. At the information board, continue straight ahead along a grassy track. As this swings round to the left you will pass see the section where you ran between the mud flats. Continue to the metal bench seat and retrace the tarmac footpath back to the beach front café.

Running along the elevated section above the mud flats before returning to the tarmac path. Photo by Julia Kelly.

ROUTE 2

Newborough Forest - Llanddwyn Island Circuit

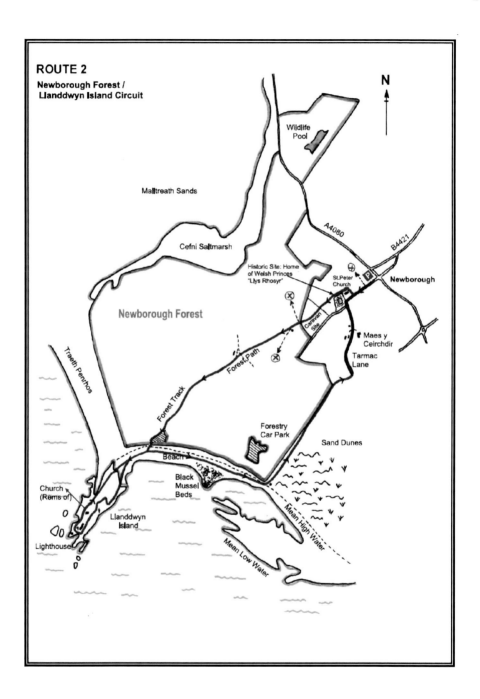

ROUTE 2
Newborough Forest /
Llanddwyn Island Circuit

N

Wildlife Pool

Malltreath Sands

A4080

B4421

Cefni Saltmarsh

Historic Site: Home
of Welsh Princes
"Llys Rhosyr"

St.Peter
Church

P

Newborough

Newborough Forest

Caravan Site

Maes y
Ceirchdir

Traeth Penrhos

Forest Path

Tarmac
Lane

Forest Track

Forestry
Car Park

Sand Dunes

Beach

Church
(Rems of)

Black
Mussel
Beds

Llanddwyn
Island

Mean High Water

Lighthouse

Mean Low Water

34

ROUTE 2: NEWBOROUGH FOREST – LLANDDWYN ISLAND CIRCUIT

DISTANCE: 7.2 Miles

ASCENT: Min. 0 metres (sea level). Max. 50 metres (at start).

TERRAIN: This excellent route consists mainly of sheltered forest tracks, grassy footpaths and open 'Blue Flag' beach running, on relatively firm sand. There are two sections of tarmac road running; at the start and at the finish. Trail or fell running shoes are a distinct advantage, but not absolutely necessary. *Please note that: the section of beach between the mainland forest area and Llanddwyn Island itself, is tidal.* During high tides the water fills from both sides and can cut the island off for several hours until it recedes. Access can be re-gained about 2 hours after high tide (approx). Depending on the tidal state and the time you choose to run, it may not be possible to include the island section. However, please do not "chance it" on the very fast rising tide. The penalty being, a wait of 2 to 3 hours. On a nice sunny day not too much of an emergency but, in the depths of winter, with very little shelter, a totally different 'kettle of fish!' If in doubt go online and check tide times for the Anglesey region.

TIME: 55 mins. to 1Hr.10 mins. approx.(depending on weather conditions, especially wind strength and direction)

START: Newborough Village, Church Street Free Car Park.

O.S MAP: 1:25,000 Sheet 263 Anglesey.

GRADIENT: The vast majority of this route is on the flat with a few sections involving short, undulating ascents and descents.

ACCESS: The whole area of Newborough Forest is managed by the Countryside Commission for Wales. Due to its historic and natural habitat significance, Llanddwyn Island and Newborough Warren are managed by the Countryside Council for Wales and designated a National Nature Reserve. Owing to the large numbers of visitors each year, there are restrictions in place, i.e., no dogs between May 1st and September 30th, no campfires or 'wild camping', and keep to designated paths and tracks at all times. A resident warden is present during the busy summer period. However, this ceases during the autumn and winter months. The whole area of Newborough Forest and its coastline is regularly used by runners, walkers, mountain bikers and horse riders. Please ensure that the by-laws and requests are observed and courtesy given to other users.

Grid References

423656	Church Street Car Park, Newborough Village.
414651	Exit from forest on to 'Ro Bach' beach area.
395635	Entrance gate to forest.
385625	Llanddwyn Lighthouse (Dis).
409631	Marker post in sand dunes.
421644	Left turning on to tarmac road passing houses.
419653	Road junction.

FGS Grading: Grading is T4 [D1, N1,T1,R1,H0]

Distance	1	6 – 12 miles
Navigation	1	Basic navigation skills needed.
Terrain	1	50 – 75% on graded track or path. 25 – 50% off track.
Remoteness	1	Countryside in fairly close proximity to habitation – at least 80% of the route within 2 miles.
Height	0	Less than 100ft per mile.

Route Description :

1. Begin the run at the free car park just off Church Street in Newborough Village (**GR 423656**). Turn right on to Church Street and run out of the village gently uphill, passing houses and a public footpath sign on your right. Ignore this sign and proceed a little further, passing the national speed limit signs, either side of the road. Just after this you will see the Church of St. Peter. Turn right here and head towards the church. An obvious metal kissing gate to the side of St. Peter's allows access to another kissing gate and a narrow path extending past the back of the church. The next section passes through a further six (!) kissing gates as one runs past a caravan park. Ahead of you lies the straight eastern fringe of Newborough Forest. After the last metal gate (please make sure this is fastened after you!), run across a grass field towards a clearly defined wooden gate/ entrance into the forest (**GR 414651**). Run the gently descending forest track (ignoring the track to your right as you emerge through the wooden gate), taking the right 'fork' at the wooden marker post with a '30' carved into it. Follow this grassy path for some way until you reach the point where it opens out and forms a 'crossroads', marked by a park bench.

Julia Kelly entering Newborough Forest at (GR 414651).
Photo: Jim Kelly

The trail opens out by the cross roads. Photo: Jim Kelly.

2. The trail now becomes wider and a lot more open. It continues south-westerly, passing a metal road barrier, as one approaches the southern edge of the forest.

3. The sea and the narrow finger of land, known as Llanddwyn Island, can now be seen through the trees as the track terminates at a car parking area. Drop down between the sand dunes and on to the beach itself *(marked as 'Ro Bach' on the map)*, turning right and aiming for the rocky outcrops that emerge out of the sand (**GR 395635**). These are the remnants of volcanic action some 570 million years ago when all this area was under the Lapetus Ocean. Their technical term is *'Pillow lavas'*. With the geology lesson over (!), and assuming the tidal state allows access, run towards the island, aiming for the large wooden display board that marks the start of the island's network of paths. A very good tourist path leads one around the island, passing a cattle grid and on to a row of old, refurbished 'Pilots Cottages' and an old iron canon.

Julia Kelly passing the Pilots Cottages as the path swings around to the Southern tip of **Llanddwyn Island.**

4. This path leads around the southern tip, passing the disused lighthouse (**GR 385625**) and up a small incline, past a cross. Further along this path are the ruins of the ancient Llanddwyn Island Church, known as *'St. Dwynwen's'*. It dates back to the early 16th C.

5. The path rises up slightly and keeps to the left. Avoid descending back towards the cattle grid here. Some wooden decking over the dunes allows one to drop down some rocky steps and on to the beach once again. Now retrace your steps past the rocky 'Pillows' and maintain an easterly direction along the fantastic, wide beach. On a warm day this is as good as anywhere else in the world! Hence, its massive popularity with visitors, especially at weekends.

6. You are heading towards a gap in the sand dunes, marked by a solitary 'Anglesey Coastal Path' wooden marker post (**GR 409631**). This isn't obvious… at all! (see

photo). However, landmarks to look out for are; the large, dark area of mussel beds visible at low tide and a high marker post/pole indicating the official forestry car park. Once located, plough through the deep sand to the top of the dunes and then descend the other side towards the eastern tree line.

7. Run along a narrow, twisty sandy path, passing through a wooden gate and on to another, allowing access to a wider forestry path through the trees. This rises gently uphill until the north-eastern corner of the forest is met. Here the path now becomes a good track/ tarmac road as it swings round to the left and past several dwellings (**GR 421644**). The landmark here is the house known as '*Maes-y-ceirchdir*', passed on your right. Continue to the top of

the tarmac road (**GR 419653**), heading straight towards the ancient remains of the 12th/13th Century home of the Welsh Princes; *'Llys Rhosyr'*

8. You will also see the Church of St. Peter once more (now on your left), as you retrace the initial road section back towards the village and Church Street car park.

Well done! You have just ticked one of the most pleasant trail routes in this region and one which is a great introduction to Newborough Forest.

ROUTE 3

Deganwy to Great Orme Circuit

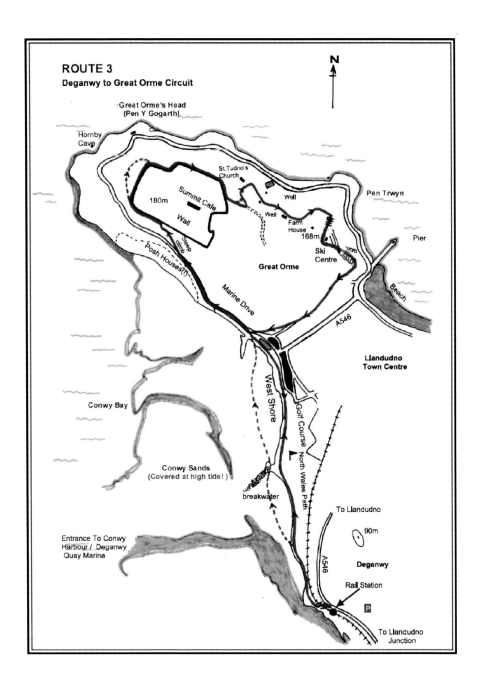

ROUTE 3
Deganwy to Great Orme Circuit

43

ROUTE 3: DEGANWY TO GREAT ORME CIRCUIT

DISTANCE: 8 Miles

ASCENT: Min. 0 metres (sea-level) @ start. Max.180 metres.

TERRAIN: A nice contrasting blend of coastal and off-road running along established footpaths, with some seaside town 'urban tarmac' thrown in for good measure. The route is very well defined with around half of it using the 'North Wales Path Route'. The track around the top of the Great Orme is well-trodden with only one or two sections becoming muddy after prolonged rain. However, being limestone, the whole headland drains and dries relatively quickly.

During the summer season, expect to 'share' sections of this route with the hordes of tourists that visit Llandudno each day, especially at weekends. Many of these 'walkers' are, let's say, 'in their senior years'. Please show courtesy at all times and allow people 'space'. The whole area is also rather more sheltered and milder than its Snowdonia counterparts. This makes for an ideal and pleasant alternative run for even the most experienced trail or fell runner.

TIME: 1 Hour 20 mins. Approx.

START: Deganwy Rail Station car park ('North Wales Path')

O.S MAP: 1:25,000 Sheet North Wales OL17.

GRADIENT: In the main, relatively level or gentle in gradient; the one exception being the hillside climb to the 'summit' of the Great Orme and the country park at its top. Although quite steep, the ascent is short lived and there is certainly no harm or shame in walking this section.

ACCESS: No known access issues. The majority of footpaths in this area are well-marked and signposted public rights of way. Please respect other users and 'give way' to them, if required to do so. Please close all gates after you.

Grid References

779791	Deganwy rail stn. car park
773806	Breakwater
772820	West Shore
762829	Steep path to the Orme
759834	Top of steep path/ limestone perimeter wall
768841	Corner of perimeter wall
769836	Junction with tarmac road
770838	Path by St.Tudno's Church
774835	Farm house with metal gate
779835	Top of Ski Centre

781829   Road into Llandudno Town Centre
772820   West Shore

FGS Grading: Grading is: T5 [D1, N1, T0, R0, H3]

Distance	1	6 – 12 miles
Navigation	1	Basic navigation skills needed
Terrain	0	75% + on graded track or path
Remoteness	0	Urban
Height	3	Over 250 ft per mile

Route Description :

1. Park in Deganwy at the railway station car park (if spaces permit **GR 779791**). If not, there are many side roads within that small area without restrictions. Begin by crossing the railway line at the manned-crossing. This will take you along a tarmac access road, past houses overlooking Conwy Sands and the entrance to the estuary. This route follows the 'North Wales Path' at this point. Run along the road until it 'fades' into a gravel path above the cobbled beach and on to West Shore. At low tide it is possible to drop down across the cobbles and pebbles and on to a very pleasant, firm, sandy beach (*see map*). This route passes the breakwater at **GR 773806** and continues across to the activity park at West Shore (**GR 772820**).

2. On reaching West Shore, by whichever route you have opted to take, run towards the Great Orme in a north westerly direction along what is known as 'Marine Drive.' This particular section of road lays claim to be the most expensive mile of 'real estate' in the whole of Wales! Continue to run gently uphill until a sign on the right (**GR 762829**) directs one up

45

Jim Kelly is approaching the breakwater between Deganwy and West Shore. Photo. Julia Kelly

a grassy incline and on to a narrow, steep grass path heading towards the lime-stone rocks at the top of the Great Orme. The views of the bay (and the 'rich folks houses'!) from up here, are superb.

3. At the top of the **path (GR 759834)** you will clearly see the high, limestone constructed perimeter

Almost at the top of the Great Orme with West Shore far below you.

wall that surrounds the Great Orme Country Park. Run alongside this following a narrow path in a clockwise direction, passing the right-

46

The Author, Jim Kelly running across the limestone pavement towards the North Westncorner of The Great Orme country park to point GR 768841. Photo. Julia Kelly.

angled northwest corner.

4. At this point (**GR 768841**), the grassy path improves and becomes a much wider track with a gravel surface. Run this south easterly where it eventually meets a narrow country lane leading to the Great Orme Mines and other 'touristy' things! At the junction with this road (**GR 769836**), turn left and run steeply downhill towards the very obvious cemetery of St. Tudno's Church. Just after the entrance to the church, there is a public footpath sign over on the right (**GR 770838**). Take this and proceed along a narrow path flanked on both sides by bushes and hedgerow. Two wooden kissing gates are passed, including a sign for "Ffynnon Powell" (Powell's Well). After continuing by some fields, a large white farm house is met with a galvanised metal gate and sign saying, "Town Centre" (**GR 774835**). Go through this gate and follow the signs which, after a few minutes, take you downhill towards some concrete steps and the top of the Llandudno Ski Centre (**GR 779835**). Follow the narrow path on the right that descends adjacent to the ski centre toboggan slide and down to their car park. Run across the car park and down the steep road that goes through the 'Happy Valley' towards Llandudno. Near the bottom, turn right and take a descending tarmac footpath that passes under the cable car wires and emerges at a road containing guesthouses and hotels on your right (**GR 781829**).

5. The easiest and most logical option here is to follow this road south westerly through the town back towards West Shore. Once arrived at West Shore again (**GR 772820**), retrace your steps back towards Deganwy via either the coastal path or, the beach. Please note that due to the state of the tides, Conwy Sands are covered at high tide, thus rendering this beach option impassable. Blame the moon and gravity! Such is life!

ROUTE 4

Newborough Forest Circular Trail

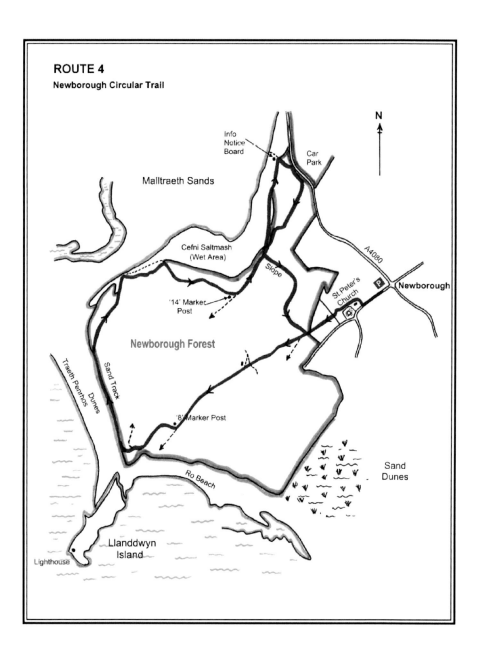

ROUTE 4
Newborough Circular Trail

N

Info Notice Board

Car Park

Malltraeth Sands

Cefni Saltmash (Wet Area)

Slope

A4080

'14' Marker Post

St Peter's Church

P

Newborough

Newborough Forest

Traeth Penthos

Dunes

Sand Track

'8' Marker Post

Ro Beach

Sand Dunes

Llanddwyn Island

Lighthouse

ROUTE 4: NEWBOROUGH FOREST CIRCULAR TRAIL

DISTANCE: 9 Miles
ASCENT: Min. 5 metres. Max.35 metres.
TERRAIN: This is the second Newborough Forest route to feature in this guide. Slightly further than Route 2, this superb trail run includes the west and north western areas of the forest. The route is entirely off road with the exception of the first ¼ mile or so on tarmac, used briefly at the beginning and end of the run. Consisting of gravel forest tracks and sandy pathways, this trail run maintains interest throughout with some wonderful views across 'Malltraeth Sands' and to the mouth of the Afon Cefni.

During wet spells, some sections of the track can get a bit boggy, particularly around the Cefni Saltmarsh area which is barely above sea level and drains quite slowly. Although this route can be done in normal running trainers, trail shoes do offer a little more 'traction' on the sand and gravel sections.

Although the route finding is relatively straightforward, it is helpful to take a copy of the OS Map, Sheet 263, with you (if possible).

TIME: 1 Hour 20 – 35 mins. approx.
START: Newborough Village car park off Church Street (Free at the time of writing!). Toilet Facilities during the summer months.
O.S MAP: 1:25,000 Sheet 263 Anglesey.
GRADIENT: Gentle gradients throughout.
ACCESS: The whole area is run and managed by the Countryside Commission for Wales. Outdoor enthusiasts are encouraged to use the area. However, please remember to obey any signs, close gates securely and respect other users. The forest gets particularly busy at weekends and during the spring and summer months.

Grid References

423656	Church Street car park, Newborough Village.
414651	Entrance gate to forest.
398640	Sharp turn right onto track.393637
393637	Small sandy path.
388648	Sandy path re-enters main forest.
391656	Cefni Saltmarsh.
405665	'T- junction'/ marker post '17'.
408661	Track on the right.
411671	Forestry Commission car park.
411653	Left turning at junction.

FGS Grading: Grading is T3 [D1, N1, T0, R1, H0]

Distance	1	6 -12 miles
Navigation	1	Basic navigation skills needed
Terrain	0	75% + on graded track or path.
Remoteness	1	Countryside in fairly close proximity to habitation – at least 80% of the route within 2 miles.
Height	0	Less than 100 ft per mile.

Route Description :

The initial part of this run is identical to Route 2; "Newborough to Llanddwyn Island Circuit".

1. Begin the run at the free car park just off Church Street in Newborough Village (**GR 423656**). Turn right on to Church Street and run out of the village, gently uphill, passing houses and a public footpath sign on your right. Ignore this sign and proceed a little further, passing the national speed limit signs either side of the road. Just after this you will see the Church of St. Peter over to your right. Turn right here and head towards the church. An obvious metal kissing gate to the side of St. Peter's allows access to another kissing gate and a narrow path extending past the rear of the church. The next section passes through a further six (!) kissing gates as one runs past a small caravan park. Ahead of you lies the straight eastern fringe of Newborough Forest. After the last metal gate, *(please make sure you close this to prevent animals escaping!)* run across a grass field towards a clearly defined wooden gate allowing entry to the forest (**GR 414651**).

2. Run the gently descending forest track, taking the right 'fork' at a wooden marker post with a number '**30**' carved into it. Follow this grassy footpath for some way until you reach the point where it opens out and forms a 'crossroads', marked by a wooden park bench. From here, the trail becomes wider and more open in character continuing in a south westerly direction. At **GR 398640** take a sharp right turn (wooden marker post with a number '**8**'

The author Jim Kelly at GR398640 making the sharp right turn of the main track.
Photo: Julia Kelly.

carved into it) and follow another forest road heading in a west to south westerly direction.

3. At its southernmost point (**GR 393637**) ignore the continuation of this track. Instead, opt for the small sandy path that leads one down towards the large area of high sand dunes that extend along 'Traeth Penrhos'. This sandy path now heads roughly north in a straight line for a mile or so, passing a large area of 'surreal' dead pine trees, either side of you, presumably the remnants of a forest fire many years ago? It is also worth taking a few moments out to locate one of the many small sandy paths that lead through the dunes to the beach. The view of Traeth Penrhos from the crest of these dunes is incredible!

**At the start of the long sandy path heading North along Traeth Penrhos.
Photo: Julia Kelly.**

4. At **GR 388648** the sandy path re-enters the forest once again emerging at a junction after half a mile or so. Take the left turn and continue running north towards the edge of the trees where the area known as 'Cefni Saltmarsh' is met (**GR 391656**). To avoid any 'wet bits' it is best to run along the drier footpath that skirts the trees, now on your right. Yet again, the coastal views here across to 'Malltraeth Sands' are superb.

5. After a short way this smaller path connects with the forest trail once again and heads in a south easterly direction. This continues through mixed trees to another 'T- junction' at **GR 405665** (wooden marker post here with a number '**17**' carved into it). Turn left and run this straight wide track as it heads northeast with fine views of the

Cefni Saltmarsh looking across towards Malltraeth Sands.

saltmarsh to your left. At **GR 408661** a track on the right is passed which heads uphill slightly. (*Remember this for later!*)

6. Continue along the path you are on for a short way until you come across a low marker post pointing to the left through the trees. Ignore the continuation of the forest track and take this narrow footpath instead. This leads all the way to the public car park at **GR 411671** via a series of sections spanned by wooden 'decking' to overcome muddy pools etc. A large information display board is also present here telling you about the area as a whole.

7. From the car park, emerge onto the A4080 and run along the footpath on the right hand side. Remain on this for 150 yards or so until a track on the right allows you to re-enter the forest. Run along this track for about half a mile until it curves and descends slightly to the point where you went through the trees at the previous low marker post. Retrace your steps back further now towards the point at which I told you to, *'remember this for later!'* Well, this is it! Now take this left turn uphill and follow the forest trail as it curves round to the south. At **GR 411653**, turn left at the junction and continue along in a straight line until you reach the point at which you entered

Wooden decked footpath, avoiding boggy areas, leading to the forestry commission car park.

Newborough Forest in the first place (**GR 414651**). All that remains now is to turn left, go back through the gate and retrace your strides, via St. Peter's Church, back to the car in Newborough Village car park.

ROUTE 5

PentraethForest to Red Wharf Bay

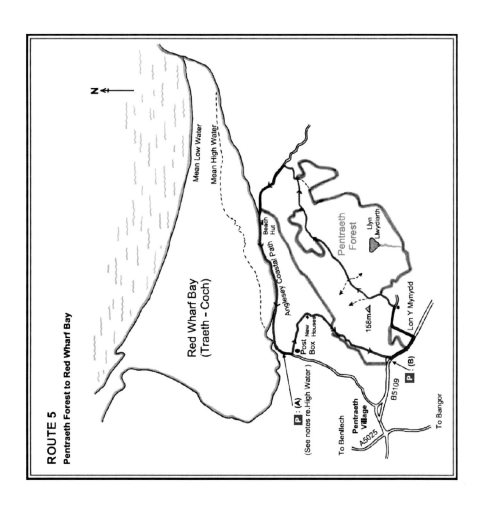

ROUTE 5
Pentraeth Forest to Red Wharf Bay

ROUTE 5: PENTRAETH FOREST TO RED WHARF BAY

DISTANCE: 5 ¼ Miles

ASCENT: Min.0 metres. Max.150 metres.

TERRAIN: This great little trail run combines the gravel tracks in Pentraeth Forest, Anglesey *(also known and 'signed' as "Red Squirrel Wood")* with the sandy path that extends across the vast tourist beach of 'Red Wharf Bay'. With the exception of some short, connecting sections on tarmac, the route is all off-road.

The terrain in the forest varies from wide open tracks to narrow, leafy pathways, the latter of which can get a bit muddy after prolonged wet spells. There are also occasional exposed tree roots in places so, beware of your footing. These can get very slippery!

The coastal element is superb, using a section of the Anglesey Coastal Path, giving far reaching views across the bay towards the tourist town of Benllech. Although not essential, trail or fell running shoes would be a distinct advantage.

TIME: 50 mins to 1 hour 10mins. approx. depending on navigation stops etc.

START: There are two possible starts: **(A).** The first is the official public car park at Red Wharf Bay **(GR 535799)**, accessed via a minor road off the B5109, east of Pentraeth Village. However, this sandy area is tidal in places! Park one's car with care!! **(B).** The second parking spot is a small lay-by, on the left, just off the B5109 at **GR 534784 (signed, "Red Squirrel Wood").** There is parking here for 2 cars. Police signs advise people not to leave any valuables on show! (common sense advice really for any car park, any time, any place!!)

O.S MAP: 1:25,000 OS Sheet Anglesey 263.

GRADIENT: Mainly gentle or flat. One or two very short, uphill sections.

ACCESS: No known access issues. Please respect signs directing the general public away from private residential dwellings where they are in close proximity to footpaths.

Grid References

534784	Route start at small lay-by off B5109.
537781	"Lon y Mynydd" country lane.
542786	Junction of continuation path.
550798	T-junction at green gates.
558796	Start of access track passing houses.
553801	Red Wharf Bay.
535799	Car park '**A**'.
538796	Access drive to new houses

FGS Grading: Grading is T3 [D0, N1, T0, R1, H1]

Distance	0	Up to 6 miles
Navigation	1	Basic navigation skills needed
Terrain	0	75%+ on graded track or path
Remoteness	1	Countryside in fairly close proximity to habitation – at least 80% of the route within 2 miles
Height	1	Over 100 ft per mile

Route Description :

For the purposes of this route description, I have used parking area "B" (GR 534784) as the starting point for this run. (At the small lay-by you cannot help but notice a footpath sign and kissing gate. All will become clear... 'eventually!')

1. From the car, run along the B5109, heading in a south easterly direction. At the top of the rise the road flattens and becomes straight. The first turning on your left is a narrow lane signed, "Lon y Mynydd" (**GR 537781**). Take this and run along it as it bends sharp right after a short distance.

Continue gently uphill until a public footpath on the left takes you up a narrow, rising track with bushes either side and a kissing gate at it's top. The narrow path now proceeds along a dry stone wall, on your right, to-wards another kissing gate. Go through the gate and opt for the gently rising, continuation path (**GR 542786**).

After a little way, this 'opens' out passing a cleared area of felled and decaying conifer trees on your right. There are some great views from here across to the distant, mainland mountains of Snowdonia. The small lake of 'Llyn Llwydiarth' is also visible below you.

**Descending the track past the area of dead and felled trees.
Photo: Julia Kelly.**

2. Run down the path to a cross-paths junction, marked by a low, overgrown rock face in front of you. Proceed along the forest track that heads uphill slightly and in a north westerly direction. This good trail now extends for some distance as it rises and drops. Eventually, at **GR 550798**, one arrives at another 'T- junction with some scruffy green gates in front of you. Turn right here and continue to run along the rising track. At a clearing on your left, opt to take the descending track through the trees down towards a vehicle track and residential houses at, **GR 558796.**

3. After a very short descent, this 'access road' to the properties joins the tarmac country lane that terminates at the spectacular beach of Red Wharf Bay **(GR 553801).** Head in a westerly direction, following the sandy 'Anglesey Coastal Path' for just over a mile, eventually reaching the car park, referred to in the *'Start Section'* as, **"A"** **(GR 535799).**

Running along the Anglesey coastal path section towards the public car park.

Above. Running along the Anglesey coastal path section towards the public car park. Below. Dramatic skies over Red Wharf Bay. Photo showing car park 'A' and its close proximity to the tidal beach. . Photos: Julia Kelly.

4. From the car park head south and cross the small road bridge over a drainage channel. Not far ahead you will come to a left turn by a red post box. Take this turning and run along the tarmac lane back up towards the steep hillside and Pentraeth Forest. At **GR 538796**, the tarmac lane gives way to an access drive to some white, new-build residential houses. At the house, follow the footpath signs to your 'right' (south westerly!) as the track rises up towards a yellow-signed property named, "**PLAS TIRION**". Another yellow sign above this says, "**FOOTPATH**" with an arrow pointing the way! (*Why do I get the feeling here that they are not at all happy with walkers wandering into their driveway and garden!?*)

5. Clear that you are on the correct route, run up the inclined path as it forms an "S-curve". At the top of the curve, another footpath sign directs you south westerly along the north west fringe of Pentraeth Forest. The path is quite narrow and, as a result, can get a touch overgrown in the summer months with bracken etc. However, after passing a derelict house on your right, the path enters the trees and widens somewhat. A short steep descent (exposed tree roots and possible mud here!) through the pine trees leads to a level path which, amazingly (!) brings you to a kissing gate. Remember, I said at the beginning of this route description to hold a thought about a "sign and a kissing gate?" Well, this is it.... and, so is you car!! You are now back exactly where you started!! Well done!

ROUTE 6

Llyn Crafnant to-Llyn Geirionydd Circuit

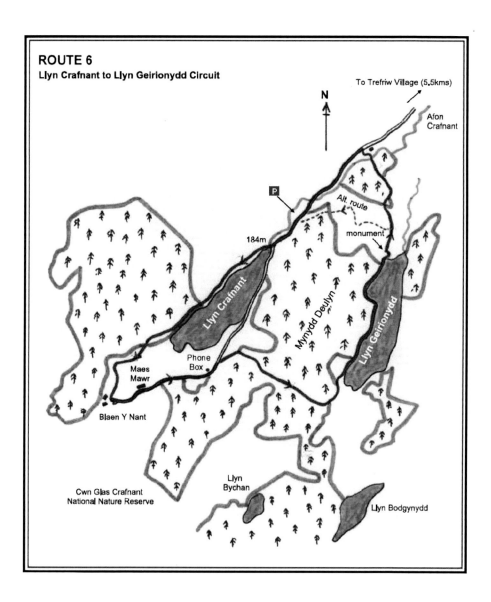

ROUTE 6
Llyn Crafnant to Llyn Geirionydd Circuit

To Trefriw Village (5.5kms)

N

Afon Crafnant

P

Alt. route

184m

monument

Llyn Crafnant

Mynydd Deulyn

Llyn Geirionydd

Phone Box

Maes Mawr

Blaen Y Nant

Cwn Glas Crafnant National Nature Reserve

Llyn Bychan

Llyn Bodgynydd

ROUTE 6: LLYN CRAFNANT TO GEIRIONYDD CIRCUIT

DISTANCE: 5 Miles
ASCENT: Min.154 metres @ start. Max.300 metres.
TERRAIN: Superbly picturesque lakes bounded on their sides by rocky crags and steep wooded hillsides consisting mainly of coniferous trees. This is a 'jewel' of a trail run in a magnificent setting. The area is also popular with walkers, rock climbers and anglers so don't expect total solitude. However, there is very much a remote, unspoilt feel to the area. Please do your bit to keep it that way.
TIME: 1 Hour 5 – 15 mins. Approx.
START: Take the minor road west of and up hill from the village of Trefriw. The lake, 'Llyn Crafnant' is signposted from Trefriw as a fishing area. Park at the Forestry Commission car park and public toilets north of Llyn Crafnant (GR 757618). At the time of writing, this car park is free of parking charges.
O.S MAP: 1:25,000 Sheet North Wales OL17.
GRADIENT: Relatively, gentle, easy lakeside trails with some sections of tarmac minor road. Steep(ish) ascent of the ridge separating the two valleys.
ACCESS: The entire area is known as Cwm Glas Crafnant National Nature Reserve. It is a component of the surrounding Cwm Crafnant Site of Special Scientific Interest (SSSI) and supports a range of habitats including woodland, marshland and cliffs. There is open access on the reserve with the exception of a fenced area which helps prevent grazing by agricultural livestock. There are no formal public footpaths and the reserve is managed by the Countryside Council for Wales. Please obey the countryside code and any special sign requests.

Grid References

757618	Forestry Commission Car Park
743607	Footpath branches to the left
738603	'Blaen y Nant'
748606	Public payphone box
764605	Llyn Geirionydd
759604	Stile
763612	Disused mine
765616	'Alternative' footpath descent to car park

FGS Grading: Grading is T2 [D0, N1, T0,R1,H0]

Distance	0	Up to 6 miles
Navigation	1	Basic navigation skills needed
Terrain	0	75% + on graded track or path
Remoteness	1	Countryside in fairly close proximity to habitation – at least 80% of the route within 2 miles.
Height	0	Less than 100 ft per mile

**Llyn Crafnant Forestry Commission car park entrance.
Photo: Julia Kelly.**

Route Description :

1. From the Forestry Commission car park at **GR 757618** turn right and follow the minor road up towards Llyn Crafnant Reservoir and the 184m spot height which marks the outflow of the Afon Crafnant. At the outflow, cross the river and run along the excellent, wide forestry track above the edge of the lake, in an anti-clockwise direction. There has been extensive tree felling on the hillside above here.

Running along the gravel track towards the South Western corner of Llyn Crafnant. Photo: Julia Kelly.

2. Continue in a south-westerly direction along this track until a smaller footpath branches off to the left at **GR 743607** and descends to a stile not attached to anything! 'Go past' the stile and continue descending through some trees until a a small footbridge and access road are met. Run along this road passing the nearby 'Blaen y Nant' climbing hut belonging to the Mynydd Climbing Club (**GR 738603**).

Go through a metal gate and run along the minor tarmac road, passing the properties 'Maes Mawr' and 'Cornel', both on your left. At **GR 748606** a BT public payphone box is met. Immediately opposite is a footpath marked with a blue square and white boot print symbol. Take this footpath as it gradually ascends the steep, wooded hillside.

3. This upward path narrows and 'darkens' as it passes through dense larch trees. However, the upward angle soon eases as one emerges at the top of the rounded ridge with the path opening out once again. The now

Crossing a small stream on the hillside ascent towards the next valley, Llyn Geirionydd. Photo: Julia Kelly.

descending path soon connects with another forestry track with leads to the second of our lakes, 'Llyn Geirionydd' (**GR 764605**). Follow the defined path as it descends towards the valley floor, crossing the forestry road in several places.

4. At **GR 759604** another stile is met. Cross this and run along the left-hand side of the lake on a narrow, waterside path. This area is very picturesque but make sure you keep your eyes in front of you because there are numerous exposed tree roots along this path. A certain degree of concentration is required here.

5. After half a mile or so the path is forced up and over some rocks, passing an old disused 'mine' on the left (**GR 763612**). The lakeside path

Descending the forestry track towards Llyn Geirionydd.
Photo: Julia Kelly.

continues past some large boulders towards the northern end of the lake where it climbs a grassy knoll with a stone monument at it top.

Pass the monument in a northerly direction following a path that descends past some more trees down towards the Afon Crafnant. Cross the river and emerge onto the minor tarmac road, taking a left turn here and running it for half a mile to the Forestry Commission car park.

A shorter variation also exists here. At **GR 765616** another path (marked 'Trefriw Trails') leads one along a narrow, undulating, stony path which emerges directly opposite the forestry car park! Although shorter by about ½ mile, this alternative line in no way detracts from the route as a whole. It's your choice. Either way, you have just completed one of the best shorter trail routes in the area. Fantastic on a warm summer's evening! Be sure to pack some food, a disposable Bar-B-Que and some beers. Locate a quiet spot and make an evening of it.... it's really idyllic!!

71

Llyn Trawsfynydd Circuit

ROUTE 7

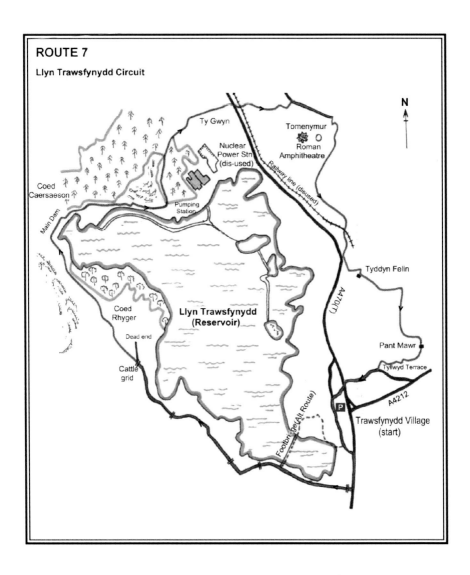

ROUTE 7

Llyn Trawsfynydd Circuit

ROUTE 7: LLYN TRAWSFYNYDD CIRCUIT

DISTANCE: 10 ½ miles
ASCENT: Min.197 metres @ start. Max.310 metres.
TERRAIN: This is a superb, long trail run that utilises a mixture of footpaths, tracks and tarmac road sections. The route is described in a clockwise direction and includes some magnificent views across the Trawsfynydd Reservoir towards the Rhinog hills and Cadair Idris. Trawsfynydd is the 3rd largest area of still water in Wales, covering some 1200 acres. The run passes the site of the, now disused nuclear power station, for which this area is well-known. In addition to this, the trail also passes the site of the remains of a Roman Fort (Castell Tomen-y-mur) with its remains of an amphitheatre, hillfort and Roman roads. In AD 78 this was one of the most remote and exposed hill forts in Wales.

This is a great, varied run especially on a warm, breezy, Summer's day with white horses on the lake. Go to it and enjoy!
TIME: 2 ½ - 3 Hours depending on navigation/ photo stops etc.
START: Trawsfynydd Village (GR 708355). There are many places to park in the village but, please do not obstruct any resident's driveways or access roads. The free parking by the medical/ recycling area in the centre of the village is probably the best spot (GR 708356).
O.S MAP: 1:25,000 Sheet North Wales OL18
GRADIENT: On the whole, with this being a 'waterside' trail, the gradients are generally quite 'shallow'. However, there are some sections to the West and North of the reservoir that have some steep grassy climbs but, nothing which is too sustained.
ACCESS: No known access issues but, please make sure you obey the country code and any requests made by MAGNOX Electricity Generating and the Trawsfynydd Visitor Centre. There are several farm gates that must be closed properly after you have passed through them.

Grid References

708356	Start at Trawsfynydd Village recycling centre.
711350	unction with the A470.
711345	Right turn in to minor road.
684360	Signed footpath after the fifth cattle grid.
685369	Coed Rhyger woodland
675376	Road over 'Main Dam'

690382	Trawsfynydd Nuclear Power Station (disused)
687378	Footpath on the left
688385	Junction with narrow, gravel footpath
691389	'Ty Gwyn Farm'
695391	A470(T) road crossing point
703392	Minor tarmac road
707388	Parking area
709373	A470(T)
712371	'Tyddyn Felin Farm'
719363	Pant Mawr'
714360	Ardudwy Terrace

FGS Grading: Grading is T6 [D1, N2, T1, R1, H1]

Distance	1	6 – 12 miles.
Navigation	2	Competent navigation skills needed.
Terrain	1	50 - 75% on graded track or path. 25 – 50% off-track
Remoteness	1	Countryside in fairly close proximity to habitation – at least 80% of the route within 2 miles.
Height	1	Over 100 foot per mile.

Route Description :

1. From Trawsfynydd take the village road south to the main A470(T) **(GR 711350)**. At the T-junction turn right and run south along this for no more than a fewnhundred yards. At **GR 711345**, turn right at the minor tarmac road and follow this as it runs alongside the South-west corner of the lake, passing several cattle grids.

It is also possible to take a footpath from the southern end of the village which 'dogleg's' its way round to the obvious metal, narrow footbridge that spans the southern end of the lake (see route map). This emerges at the minor tarmac road just before the 2nd cattle grid, thus eliminating the need to run along the A470. However, make sure that any loose items (especially keys!) carried in pockets are secured with zips or similar. The 'wooden planks' over this bridge have gaps between them! Anything dropped would most likely fall into the very deep water below you!

At the fifth (!) cattle grid **(GR 684360)** the tarmac road terminates. Branch off left and follow the multi-signed, ascending, narrow, rocky footpath that runs above the trees of 'Coed Rhyger' **(GR 685369)**, towards the lake's North-west corner and the impressive main dam

| Jim Kelly running along the pleasant path above Coed Rhyger. |

(GR 675376). *(Make sure you do not confuse this with the signed, rising path just before this at GR 685358. This heads West towards 'Cwm Moch'... definitely not where you want to be!)*

The views throughout this section are tremendous and well worth a 'get-your-breath-stop!'

2. This stony path now descends and curves its way passing over the dam *(make sure you have a look over the wall!)*. A rising, pleasant tarmac lane through the trees now heads towards the famous 'Trawsfynydd Nuclear Power Station' at **GR 690382,** with its huge, twin reactor buildings.

A rocky section en route to the main dam.

The twin MAGNOX nuclear reactor buildings destined for decommissioning in 2088!   Photo: Julia Kelly

3. Before the reactor buildings, at **GR 687378** a path on the left takes one in a Northerly direction up through some pine woodlands above the power station. After passing through a second gate, a vague, signed path on the right descends through the dense pine trees (exposed tree roots – care!) to **GR 688385** where it meets a narrow gravel path. Turn left here and run a short distance to another gate, where a stile on the right gives access to a grassy area next to a huge, very obvious electricity pylon. This connects with a good, stony farm track, passing the farm, 'Ty Gwyn' **(GR 691389).**

Having descended through the pine woods, Jim now takes the good track towards Ty Gwyn and the A470.

4. From 'Ty Gwyn', head Eastwards towards the A470 trunk road. With care, cross the A470 **(GR 695391)** and locate the signed footpath directly opposite the road. This next section of the run is decidedly uphill so, pace yourself accordingly.

Cross the disused, railway bridge which allows access up rising fields, following the course of an ancient Roman road. This continues to head steeply uphill, emerging at a minor road at **GR 703392**.

5. At the minor road, turn right and run along this for approximately 600 yards, terminating at a parking area (**GR 707388**) and the site of the Roman Amphitheatre; 'Tomen y mur'. Depending on whether you have spent a few minutes here pretending to be 'Russell Crowe', locate the path ('Sarn Helen') that now leads one in a South-westerly direction, yet again, towards the A470 at **GR 709373**. Although it is feasible to run on the A470 South for approximately 1 mile to Trawsfynydd Village, it is more 'in-keeping' (and pleasurable!) to take the rising continuation road that leads up to 'Tyddyn Felin Farm' at **GR 712371** (please make sure you close any gates you use here).

Remain on this track past Tyddyn Felin as it climbs the hillside to the 270 metre contour and some derelict farm cottages by an old slate quarry. Continue steeply up a small, grassy valley emerging at a stile in

Passing the derelict cottages just before the steep climb up towards the short moorland section that leads to Pant Mawr.

the corner of a wall (*ignore the wooden ladder stile on your right prior to this!*), which gives access to an area of 'tussocky' moorland (310m). A vague, but signed, rising footpath swings around and, eventually, down to 'Pant Mawr' (**GR 719363**).

6. Here a good, wide access track now descends towards 'Ardudwy Terrace' at **GR 714360**. At Ardudwy Terrace, join the minor tarmac road that descends steeply towards Trawsfynydd Village and the cross roads with... yes, you've guessed, the A470... again! A short uphill run through the village is all that remains straight back towards your parked car at the recycling bins. Well done!

If you are in need of refreshment, there is a convenience store down in the centre of the village selling chilled drinks and snacks etc.

Bodysgallen to Little Orme Circuit

ROUTE 8

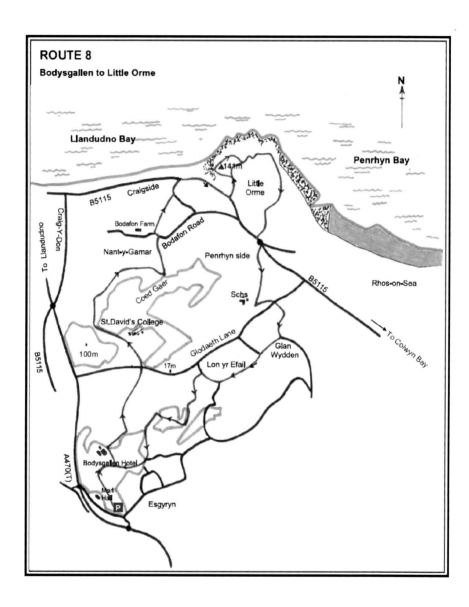

ROUTE 8
Bodysgallen to Little Orme

N

Llandudno Bay

Penrhyn Bay

▲141m

Little Orme

B5115   Craigside

Craig-Y-Don

To Llandudno

Bodafon Farm

Bodafon Road

Nant-y-Gamar

Penrhyn side

Coed Gaer

Schs

B5115

Rhos-on-Sea

St.David's College

To Colwyn Bay

Glodaeth Lane

Glan Wydden

100m

17m   Lon yr Efail

B5115

Bodysgallen Hotel

A470(T)

Marl Hall

P

Esgyryn

ROUTE 8: BODYSGALLEN TO LITTLE ORME CIRCUIT

DISTANCE: 8.5 Miles

ASCENT: Min. 7 metres @ start. Max. 141 metres.

TERRAIN: This very pleasant trail run combines undulating pasture and ancient woodland with the limestone coastal headland known as, the Little Orme. Although much smaller than its nearby 'relation', the Great Orme (see Route 3), it possesses a particular charm of its very own. Superb views of Penrhyn Bay towards the towns of Rhos-on-Sea and Colwyn Bay. The majority of this run is on public footpaths with several short 'linking' sections on tarmac. Some of the initial field sections can become quite muddy after prolonged spells of rain. The 'clayey' limestone soil can get quite 'sticky!' There are one or two sections that are 'rocky' in nature. Take care on these, as they can become slippery.

TIME: 1 Hour 45 mins. Approx. allowing for navigation stops.

START: At the Marl Hall Woods free parking area, just off the A470, between Marle Hall and the village of Esgyryn, Grid Ref. 800786.

O.S MAP: 1:25,000 Sheet North Wales OL17.

GRADIENT: Generally, gently undulating limestone countryside with several steep but, short ascents and descents.

ACCESS: No known access issues. However, the area of woods known as Marl Hall, has SSSI designation on account of the rare plant species found here. There are also requests to keep all dogs on leads crossing the land adjacent to Bodysgallen Hall Hotel. Please respect these requests.

Grid References

800786 Car parking area and start of the route
801793 Stepped wall stile by Bodysgallen Hotel
804802 Road crossing
800805 St. David's College access road
801813 Road/ track junction
804816 Bodafon Road crossing
808823 B5115
813825 Little Orme Summit Trig Point
817816 Roundabout
816818 Schools
820805 Glanwydden
806796 Goedlodd
799792 Marl Hall Woods Nature Reserve

FGS Grading: Grading is T4 [D1, N1, T0, R1, H1]

Distance	1	6 – 12 miles
Navigation	1	Basic navigation skills needed
Terrain	0	75%+ on graded track or path
Remoteness	1	Countryside in fairly close proximity to habitation – at least 80% of the route within 2 miles
Height	1	Over 100 ft per mile

Route Description :

From the A55 take the A470 towards Llandudno. At the first roundabout take the minor road uphill towards the village of Esgyryn. Keep left and park in the free car park next to Marl Hall Woods.

1. Run from the car park using the good public footpath (known locally as 'Nun's Walk') through Marl Hall Woods, passing the natural spring of 'Ffynnon Well'. Climb the wooded hillside via the 'Jacob's Ladder' path to a stile in a wall which leads one over an open field, adjacent to Bodysgallen Hall Hotel. At the other side of the field opt for a left turn onto a good track that heads towards the hotel. At **GR 801793** a stepped wall stile accesses another footpath that leads past the wooded area known as, 'Eastern Covert'. After a short distance, a left branching path heads north across fields (sometimes quite muddy!) to the 'B'-road, 'Glodaeth Lane'.

Ascending the track through Marl Hall Wood towards Bodysgallen Hall Hotel.
Photo : Julia Kelly

2. Cross the road with care and continue north westerly across another large arable field, gently rising to the access driveway for St. David's College (**GR 800805**). Just beyond the 'white house', a footpath on the right leads past the rear of the property to another path. This heads west and then swings north, narrowing as it rises steeply up the rocky, limestone hillside. The views looking west towards Llandudno and the Great Orme are truly superb!

As the top of the hill flattens, follow the descending, signed path towards 'Nant y Gamar'. Take care here as there are several other 'paths' in this vicinity.

3. At **GR 801813** a road/ track junction is met. Whilst it is possible to take the left descending lane northwards towards Craig y Don, turn right instead and run along the top of Nany y Gamar and descend through woods to emerge on 'Bodafon Road' by Bodafon Hall Farm.

4. Turn right here and run along Bodafon Road. Just beyond the farm, a footpath heads across the edge of a field to a metal kissing gate and some nice residential houses. Go straight ahead to emerge on to the B5115 Llandudno Bay Road. Cross the road and take a right and run along the rising pavement towards the Little Orme, which now rises a short distance ahead of you.

5. At **GR 814821**, a steeply rising footpath takes one towards the top of the Little Orme at 141 metres. Several tracks exist around here, which lead to the rocky summit and its Trig Point. From the summit descend the grassy track that heads in an easterly direction towards some large quarried areas. There are some big drops around here so exercise a degree of care. Run across a large, flat grassy area in a southerly direction towards a new galvanised kissing gate. This allows access to a descending, grassy 'incline'.

6. Descend this with care, arriving at a good 'tourist' track that leads to a housing estate. Run through the estate, emerging at a roundabout on the B5115 (**GR 818816** – shops here for refreshment, if required?). Cross over the roundabout and follow a minor road south which, after a short distance, connects with a good public footpath. This passes 'Glanwyddan School' at **GR 816809** and emerges, once again, on to Glodaeth Road.

Running in the evening sunshine towards the summit of The Little Orme with Colwyn Bay in the distance. Photo: Julia Kelly

7. Now turn left and run a very short distance to a public footpath on the opposite side of the road. Follow this to Glanwydden and connect with the country lane leading towards 'Lon yr Efail' at **GR 811802** where another footpath is followed over fields to 'Goedlodd' at **GR 806795**. The path now runs through some trees before meeting the earlier path you ran along leading towards St. David's College. One can now either retrace their strides back to Bodysgallen Hotel or, head in a southerly direction to emerge at the same point above Marl Hall Woods.

8. All that remains is to descend the Marl Hall stage and follow the good path back yo your parked vehicle at Esgyryn.

ROUTE 9

Holy Island, Anglesey

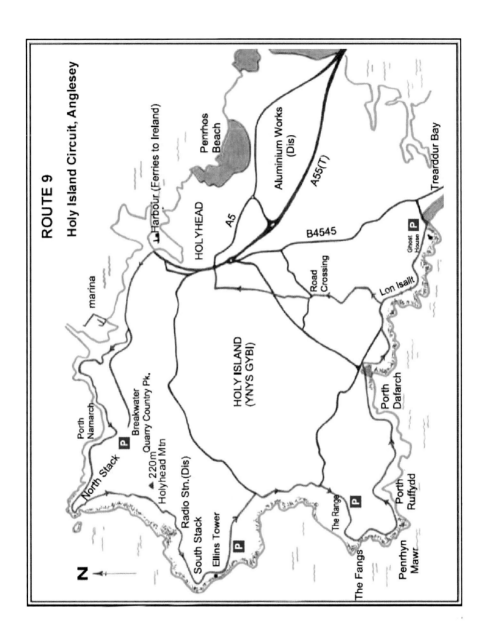

ROUTE 9

Holy Island Circuit, Anglesey

ROUTE 9: HOLY ISLAND, ANGLESEY (Ynys Mon)

DISTANCE: 14 Miles
ASCENT: Min. 0 metres ('sea-level') @ start. Max.160 metres (220m if you include an optional ascent of Holyhead Mountain) .
TERRAIN: This 'spectacular', long, coastal trail run includes all the things that make this region of Anglesey such a magnet for casual tourists and outdoor enthusiasts alike. On a warm Spring or, Summer's day, the landscape and terrain is definitely '5-Star'!

However, it is quite an open, exposed area and thus, can present the trail runner with sudden changes in weather conditions. In particular, strong westerly and north-westerly winds coming straight off the Irish Sea are often accompanied by, yes, you've guessed, rain and mist!

Although this trail run is mainly on good, defined paths and tracks, there are some sections which are quite narrow, rocky and exposed, above imposing cliffs where the sea is over 300 feet + below you! All these factors combined make this route one for the experienced trail runner only, who possesses the necessary stamina, navigational skills and ability required to tackle a route of this length.

However, if you match these criteria and feel confident, 'go for it!' You will be amply rewarded with great views and positions. Just make sure you take a camera in your hydration pack!
TIME: 2 Hours 45 mins.to 3 hours Approx. (depending on stops and detours etc.)
START: Trearddur Bay pay & display car park (opposite the 'ghost house!'), Grid ref. 252791.
O.S MAP: 1:25,000 Sheet North Wales Sheet 262.
GRADIENT: Generally long, shallow gradients in both ascent and descent. However, there are some steeper ascents in the north-western section of the route around Holyhead Mountain and above Gogarth Bay.
ACCESS: Much of this area is controlled by the Nature Conservancy Council on account of many areas having high importance in terms of geological, botanical or biological interest. These controls and restrictions apply mainly to rock climbers. For the 'trail runner', there are no known access issues. However, in the interests of all 'users', it is important that no environmental damage is inflicted. Please obey the Country Code and any 'signed' requests from landowners, particularly if running with your dog(s) in this area.

Grid References
252791 Trearddur Bay pay & display car park

242797 Track after Porth y Post' beach
244807 Minor road by Trearddur Bay Golf Course
244812 Housing estate
245823 Centre of Holyhead
237833 Anglesey Coastal Path
215841 North Stack
217829 Summit path to Holyhead mountain
205824 Steep, stepped path towards 'Ellin's Tower'
217815 'T' junction
217798 'Porth Ruffydd'
234799 'Porth Dafarch'

FGS Grading: Grading is T7 [D2, N2,T1, R2 ,H0]

Distance	2	12 – 18 miles
Navigation	2	Competent navigation skills needed
Terrain	1	50 – 75% on graded track or path. 25 – 50% off track.
Remoteness	2	Countryside not in close proximity to habitation – less than 20% of the route within 2 miles.
Height	0	Less than a 100 ft per mile.

The Author in full-flight, running down the narrow path with Ellin's Tower & South Stack light house in the background. Photo: Julia Kelly

Route Description :

Begin this trail run at the busy tourist village of Trearddur Bay, popular with powerboat and jet ski enthusiasts. From Easter onwards, this village gets extremely busy. There are several large pay & display car parks. The village roads tend to have 'time waiting' signs so check before you leave your vehicle. For the purposes of this route description, I have chosen the car park just north of the beach area, opposite the 'promontory' occupied by the dark, creepy-looking house; known locally as, the 'Ghost House!' However, feel free to choose your own 'spot' by all means.

1. From the car park run in a westerly direction along the coast road, 'Lon Isallt', passing the Ghost House on your left. This narrow road weaves and wends its way around the many rocky coves and inlets. Right from the start, this route is very picturesque and this is just a starter for much greater things to come over the next 14 miles!

The Author Jim Kelly running past the 'Ghost House' somewhat faster
than usual !!!   Photo: Julia Kelly.

At **GR 242797**, just beyond 'Porth y Post' beach, take the track on the right heading across open grassland northwards and adjacent to Trearddur Bay Golf Course. At **GR 244807** a minor road is met. Turn left on to the road and then, turn immediately right and follow a footpath that leads to a housing estate at **GR 244812**.

2. Run through the houses (not literally!), cross the secondary road and continue running northwards towards the centre of Holyhead (**GR 245823**). In the town centre, turn right a follow one of the roads that leads down to the main A5154, harbour road. Turn left and run along this as it runs parallel to the harbour, the 'home' of the super-fast, HSS Stena Line Ferry to Dublin. At the end of this road, turn left and follow the continuation road in a westerly direction past the Lifeboat Station and Holyhead Marina. Near to its end, you will see a large sign directing motorists to Breakwater Quarry Country Park. Take this road and follow it for a short distance until you reach a sign on the right pointing to the Anglesey Coastal Path (**GR 237833**).

Follow the good path past the enormous harbour wall that extends out into the Irish Sea and continue west towards 'North Stack', at **GR 215841**.

Running along the spectacular Anglesey Coastal Path towards North Stack. Photos: Julia Kelly.

You may notice a bit of a 'network' of paths and tracks as you approach the North Stack area. Don't worry, just keep heading upwards, following the Coastal Path signs towards Holyhead Mountain, in a southerly direction. At **GR 217829**, an obvious path leads up towards its summit at 220m. It is entirely optional here if you fancy expending the extra effort to run a detour to the summit trig point.

3. Back at the summit path junction the route now swings Southwest, high above the cliffs of Gogarth Bay, famous for its wealth of rock climbing history. The views

Heading towards Holyhead Mountain with North Stack in the background.
Photo: Julia Kelly

from here across the Irish Sea towards South Stack are simply stunning. On a clear day the Irish Coast can be made out, approximately 50 miles away on the horizon. The next leg of your run approaches the famous 'South Stack Lighthouse' and the impressive Red and Yellow Wall sea cliffs. From the minor road at **GR 205824** descend the steep, stepped path towards 'Ellin's Tower', owned by the RSPB and used as a bird observatory.

The narrow path now continues in front of Ellin's Tower and along the 'rim' of the sea cliffs with the waves some 300ft+ below you. Signs along this stretch 'remind' you of the drop! Very reassuring!

On a serious note though, a strong, 'Westerly' wind can produce powerful up-draughts here so, care is required. If in doubt or, you suffer from a fear of heights, this exposed section can be avoided by following the minor road in its entirety.

Even running can be dangerous! Photo: Julia Kelly.

4. At the end of the minor road from South Stack (**GR 217815**) a T-junction is met. Turn right here and run along the twisting country lane in a southerly direction. At **GR 218806** one reaches an access track leading to another sign-posted parking area. From the car park, run along the Anglesey Path passing through an area marked as 'The Range' on the OS Map. The moorland path now weaves its way around the rocky coastline again. Depending on the state of the tide, you may be fortunate enough to witness the 'tidal over-fall' known as 'The Fangs'. Caused by a clash of the tides and an underwater reef, the ensuing salt-water battle can create a massive area of turbulence and standing waves. Great if you are a seal catching Mackerel but not so good if you are an inexperienced skipper of a boat! Several small and large craft have been claimed here over the years.

Continue past the deep inlet known as 'Porth Ruffydd' (**GR 217798**) accessed by a steep, stepped path; a great beach for a summer's evening Bar-B-Que! Now run in an easterly direction eventually arriving at the popular tourist beach of 'Porth Dafarch', **GR 234799**.

The final stages of the run include the small tourist beach of Porth Dafarch. Photo: Julia Kelly

5. Follow the tarmac track above the beach and proceed along the coastal path, which, after a short loop, meets the 'Lon Isallt' road again leading back to Trearddur Bay. Follow this and retrace your running steps back to your vehicle at the pay & display car park, overseen by the 'ghost house'. Apart from giving 'Nosferatu' a celebratory wave, give yourself a big pat on the back. You have just 'ticked' one of the best trail runs in the whole of Wales!

ROUTE 10

Gwydyr Forest Trail

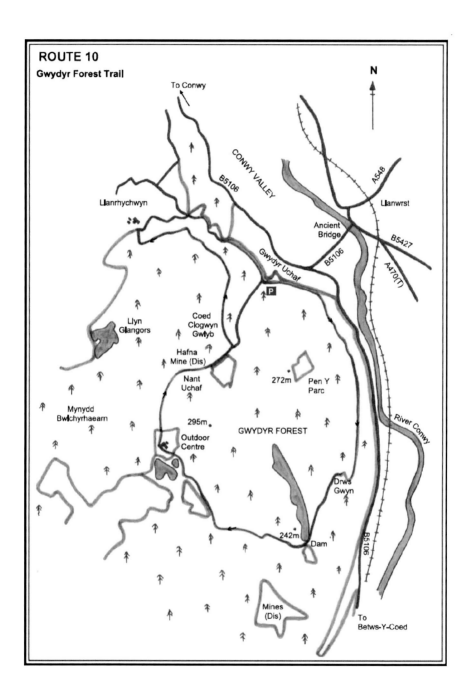

ROUTE 10
Gwydyr Forest Trail

N

To Conwy

CONWY VALLEY

B5106

A548

Llanrhychwyn

Llanwrst

Ancient
Bridge

B5427

Gwydyr Uchaf

B5106

A470(T)

P

Coed
Clogwyn
Gwlyb

Llyn
Glangors

Hafna
Mine (Dis)

Nant
Uchaf

272m

Pen Y
Parc

Mynydd
Bwlchyrhaearn

295m

GWYDYR FOREST

River Conwy

Outdoor
Centre

Drws
Gwyn

242m

Dam

B5106

Mines
(Dis)

To
Betws-Y-Coed

ROUTE 10: GWYDYR FOREST TRAIL

DISTANCE: 8 ½ Miles

ASCENT: 50 Min. metres @ start. Max. 280 metres.

TERRAIN: This is a superb forest trail run in a very popular region of Snowdonia. The tracks are all good with stable surfaces. There are many 'coloured' way-marker posts for walkers and mountain bikers. It is the 'home' to the 'MARIN Trail, a 25km mountain bike route through these forests. The views over the Conwy Valley towards the town of Llanwrst are superb. There is plenty of scope to either lengthen or shorten this run as the mood takes you. However, as with a lot of trails in dense forests, it is easy to get disorientated so, map navigation skills are essential.

TIME: 1 Hour 45 mins. Approx. (depending on stops)

START: From the town of Llanwrst, take the B5106 over the Afon Conwy. Park vehicles at 'Saw Bench' Forestry Commission car park at GR 795609 (free at the time of going to press).

O.S MAP: 1:25,000 Sheet North Wales OL17.

GRADIENT: Gentle to moderate.

ACCESS: No known access issues however, please obey all Forestry Commission requests. This area is very popular with walkers, runners and mountain bike enthusiasts. Let us maintain this.

Grid References

795609 Saw Bench Forestry Commission Car Park
797589 Narrow, rising track
795587 3 way junction
794584 Llyn y Parc
786585 Disused reservoir
779593 Outdoor pursuits centre
781601 Hafna Mine
778619 Tal Isaf
789611 Grey Mare's Tail waterfall

FGS Grading: Grading is T6 [D1, N2,T0, R2, H1]

Distance	1	6 - 12 miles
Navigation	2	Competent navigation skills needed
Terrain	0	75% ⏐ on graded track or path
Remoteness	2	Countryside not in close proximity to habitation – less than 20% of the route within 2 miles
Height	1	Over 100 ft per mile

Route Description :

1. From the Mainc Lifio 'Saw Bench' Forestry Commission Wales car park at **GR 795609**, run in a southerly direction past the metal access gate, taking the wide forestry track through Coed Carreg y-gwalch.

Remain on this as it rises gently for the next mile or so. At **GR 797589** the track narrows and rises more sharply, flattening out at the 200metre contour by 'Drws Gwyn'.

Jim & Julia Kelly at the point where the track narrows and rises towards 'Drws Gwyn'.

2. At the 214m 'spot height' (**GR 795587**) a 3-way junction is met. Take the left turn and follow the descending track to the dam and outflow of the picturesque, 'Llyn y Parc' (**GR 794584**).

Passing the lake of Llyn-y-Parc

3. After the lake continue along the rising forestry track. There is an alternative signed footpath here on the right (not the Marin Trail!) that rises through the trees. However, this is very boggy in places so, unless you yearn for wet, muddy feet, it's maybe wise to remain on the main track! This is followed in a westerly direction towards 'Coedmawr' and a small disused reservoir at **GR 786585**. At the disused reservoir continue to ascend the track. There are superb views here across to the mountains around Betws y Coed and Capel Curig. After a couple of hundred metres, a steeply rising footpath on the right takes one along the tree line, passing a large residential bungalow on the right. Follow this, now on a wide track, as it descends to another junction with several ways on. Take the right turn along a good vehicular track towards Llyn Sarnau tourist car park and Nant Bwlch yr Haearn Outdoor Pursuits Centre at **GR 779593**.

4. At the tourist car park turn right and connect with the tarmac country lane and follow it north as it descends to the 'viewpoint' and parking area at 'Hafna mine' (disused), **GR 781601**. This Victorian relic of lead mining days gone-by is quite interesting and worth spending a few minutes having a 'nose around'! Back on the country lane, continue for another ¼ mile to an open area with fields and dwellings. Just after a house sign 'Llecyn Coediog', a gated forestry track on the left is followed gently

Hafna Mine

downhill at first and then uphill again as it curves its way around the forest in a westerly direction.

This soon connects with a track that leads to the houses in the hamlet of Llanrhychwyn and Tal Isaf at **GR 778619**. Here a signpost directs one south east towards Llanwrst along another tarmac lane. This steeply descending road now leads you straight back to the Saw Bench car park. Just before the car park you will run past the stile that gives access to the 'Grey Mare's Tail' waterfalls. As it is at the end of your run, you may wish to descend the steep path down to its base… having said that, after 8 ½ miles of running another great trail run… maybe not!?

ROUTE 11

Conwy Mountain Trail

ROUTE 11
Conwy Mountain Trail

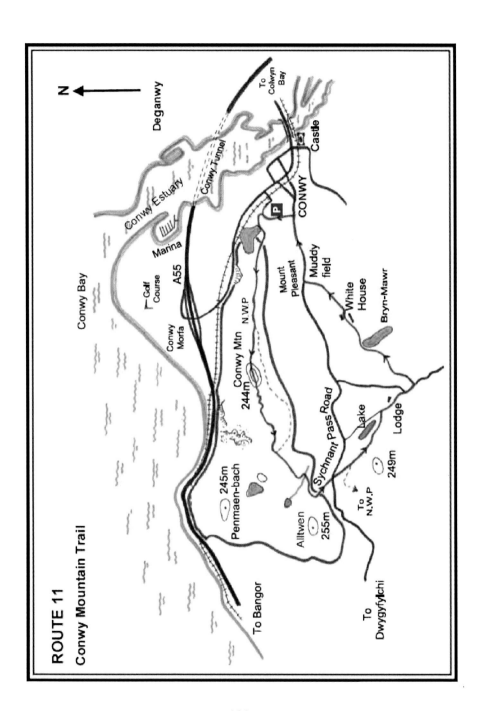

ROUTE 11: CONWY MOUNTAIN TRAIL

DISTANCE: 5 Miles
ASCENT: Min. 7 metres @ start. Max. 244 metres.
TERRAIN: On a clear day, this trail has to rate as one of the finest ways to view the North Wales Coastline and the Conwy Estuary. Fine, open, elevated positions are present throughout its five mile distance.

It also gives the trail runner an extremely varied route; from rugged, rocky mountain terrain to gently angled pasture land. Route finding is fairly straightforward with plenty of signs marking the way. However, a copy of the relevant O.S. Map, sheet OL17 would be useful.

The majority of this trail is on reasonably good public footpaths. There are some rocky sections across the summit of Conwy Mountain (Mynydd y Dref) as one runs over the historic remains of 'Castell Caer Lleion', an Iron Age fort that dates back approximately 2000 years.

TIME: 1 Hour 10 mins. Approx.
START: Park cars at Cadnant Park Road (GR 778777) in Conwy Town. Please park 'sympathetically' making sure that resident's access to properties is not obstructed in any way.
O.S MAP: 1:25,000 Sheet North Wales OL17.
GRADIENT: The first half of this trail run is mainly uphill, steep in places. However, from the summit of Conwy Mountain the angles are generally all descending or on level ground.
ACCESS: There are no known access restrictions. The area is managed between Conwy Countryside Service and Pensychnant Nature Reserve & Farm. However, there are plenty of signs requesting that dogs be kept on leads especially during the lambing season and that gates are 'closed' after you. Please take the time to respect these simple requests.

Grid References

778777 Cadnant Road (parking)
763778 Split in the footpath
760778 Conwy Mountain Summit 244m.
733776 Junction of footpaths
749773 Stream crossing
750770 Top of 'The Sychnant Pass'
755766 Small lake area
758764 'Lodge'

764766 'Bryn-mawr'
767769 Country lane
772775 Mount Pleasant
770775 'Sychnant Pass Road'

FGS Grading: Grading is T5 [D0, N1, T0, R1, H3]

Distance	0	Up to 6 miles
Navigation	1	Basic navigation skills needed
Terrain	0	75% + on graded track or path
Remoteness	1	Countryside in fairly close proximity to habitation – at least 80% of the route within 2 miles
Height	3	Over 250 ft per mile

Route Description :

1. From the A457, heading in to Conwy and, depending on whether you are approaching from either east or west, locate the narrow road that crosses the railway line at **GR 778777** and leads in to the Cadnant housing estate. It is possible to park just after the railway bridge, on the 'residential' road. From Cadnant Road, run for a short distance in a northerly direction through the estate, taking a right turn towards the North Wales Path at **GR 776778**.

2. Continue up the tarmac road until a large, obvious access gate is reached on the right hand side. From here, a delightful rising path is followed through trees and on to 'open countryside'. This continues and eventually 'dissolves' in to a grassy track that rises more steeply towards the flanks of Conwy Mountain.

Jim and Julia Kelly on the approach to Conwy Mountain. Conwy town and the Conwy Estuary are clearly visible in the far distance.

At **GR 763778** the grassy path splits. Take the right hand branch that ascends a narrow path, passing an isolated rock tower over to your right. The views throughout this stretch are magnificent!

Eventually, the path begins to flatten, which indicates you are reaching the top at last! A short uphill run across grass and low heather tussocks, places you at the summit of Conwy Mountain (244m/ **GR 760778**) and the historic remains of 'Castell Caer Hill Fort'.

Crossing the summit of Conwy Mountain amongst the remains of Castell Caer Hill Fort.

108

3. Continue westerly, descending over rocks and rubble **to GR 733776.** There is a junction of several paths here. Take the widest one heading south westerly, slightly uphill at first, then steeply descending in a straight line to a small stream crossing (dries up in warm weather!) at **GR 749773.** Use stepping stones to cross this and follow the path rightwards. After a short distance, a steeply descending tarmac road is reached and followed down to the car park at the top of 'The Sychnant Pass' **(GR 750770).**

Jim and Julia Kelly approaching the Sychnant Pass car park amidst spectacular rocky terrain.

4. The rocky terrain around here is quite spectacular with superb views towards the village of Dwygyfylchi, situated in the valley below.

Cross over the road and continue running along the gated path in a south easterly direction, passing a small lake/ marshy area at **GR 755766.**

The terrain is quite flat and open here. At the gravel access road turn right and follow it towards the 'Lodge' at **GR 758764.** After the lodge one reaches a minor tarmac road and a very nice property with its own lake.

The gravel access road running towards the Lodge at GR 758764.

Follow the minor road past the house to a sign posted public footpath is reached on the left (metal kissing gate). The path is narrow at first but soon opens out across wide fields, heading towards a wooded hillside marked as 'Bryn-mawr' at **GR 764766**. At Bryn-mawr an access road is reached via another kissing gate. Turn right here and follow the road past some very impressive, large country houses. At **GR 767769** yet another small country road is met. Turn right and immediately left on to another public footpath across fields towards 'Mount Pleasant' at **GR 772775**. Be warned, these fields can become muddy in wet weather due to livestock (horses mainly!). However, it is possible to deviate from the path and pick a drier, 'cleaner' way higher up the field.

5. At **GR 770775** Sychnant Pass Road is met. Turn right and follow this down towards Conwy town. After half a mile or so turn left into Cadnant Road once more and follow it as it descends past the point where you turned onto the North Wales Path. Turn the corner and your car is only a few more strides away.

ROUTE 12

Lleyn Peninsula Coastal Path

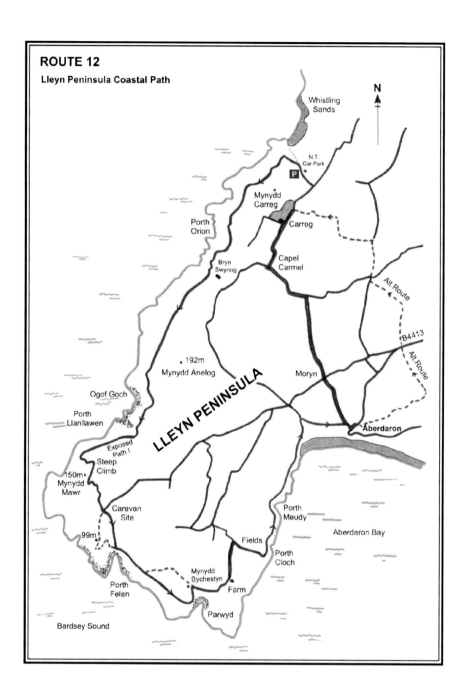

ROUTE 12: LLEYN PENINSULA COASTAL PATH

DISTANCE: 10 Miles

ASCENT: Min. 40metres @ start. Max. 110 metres.

TERRAIN: For the trail runner, this unspoilt south west spur of North Wales presents some of the finest coastal terrain one could wish for. With the exception of the return stretch from the pretty coastal village of Aberdaron to the car park at Whistling Sands, via a pleasant country lane, this trail is run entirely on the excellent Lleyn Coastal Path. The surface consists of a combination of short grass and 'clayey', compacted soil and stones. There are one or two sections where natural springs resurge and cause the path to become a touch boggy. The views are magnificent throughout and compare favourably to those experienced during the Holy Island Trail (Route 9) on Anglesey. However, being a peninsula, this area can be prone to strong South-westerly winds so, it may be wise to check out a localised weather forecast from the internet before committing to this route. Also, from a safety point of view, it's worth pointing out that one's mobile phone will most likely go into 'roaming' mode and automatically switch to 'O2 IRL', the Irish Service! Ireland is barely 50 miles across the sea with an uninterrupted signal. On a warm sunny day it would be ideal to run this trail in the morning and then spend the afternoon soaking up the sun at the stunning Whistling Sands with its shallow, clear blue water... bliss! Even trail running can involve some pure indulgence!

TIME: 2 ¼ - 2 ¾ Hours approx. depending on navigation and refreshment stops.

START: From the B4417 follow signs to Whistling Sands. Begin this route at Whistling Sands National Trust car park at GR 166295. The parking charge, at the time of going to press, is £1.50. The car park is attended and the money goes to a good cause.

O.S MAP: 1:25,000 Sheet North Wales 253.

GRADIENT: This route is gently undulating throughout, as it contours the coastal cliffs and inlets. There are several steep sections during the first half which ascend Mynydd Anelog and Mynydd Mawr. Depending on one's ability, these sections can be walked if prefered.

ACCESS: Much of this route lies on National Trust land. There are no known access issues or restrictions. Please take notice of the Trust's usual by-law requests, i.e. control of dogs and do not drop litter etc. It's a beautiful area. Let's do our bit to keep it that way.

Grid References

166295	Start at National Trust car park, Whistling Sands
157287	Porthorion
150275	Footpath 'flattens'
146264	Porth Llanllawen
140262	Narrow, exposed path
140259	Mynydd Mawr viewpoint 150m.
143257	Car park
142252	Mynydd Gwyddel
144250	Porth Felen
154244	Parwyd
153246	Mynydd Bychestyn
158246	Farm
158251	Footpath to Porth Cloch
172265	Left turn to Whistling Sands/Porthorion
164292	Mynydd Carreg

(Alternative finish):

182268	Left turn
179274	B4413
175282	Cross roads
176287	Path heads due West
166291	Minor road below Mynydd Carreg

FGS Grading: Grading is T8 [D1, N2, T1, R2, H2]

Distance	1	6 – 12 miles
Navigation	2	Competent navigation skills needed.
Terrain	1	50 – 75% on graded track or path. 25 – 50% off track
Remoteness	2	Countryside not in close proximity to Habitation – less than 20% of the route within 2 miles.
Height	2	Over 125 ft per mile

Route Description :

1. Begin this trail run at the National Trust car park, just South of Whistling Sands Beach at **GR 166295**. From the car park, head towards the public toilets and a carved wooden sign saying, 'Coastal Path'. This immediately brings you out above Whistling Sands with superb views across the cove or, 'porth' as they are known in Wales. Now follow the gently angled, grassy path Southwestwards as it contours the impressive rocky coastline.

The splendour of Whistling Sands Beach.

At **GR 157287** one runs past the inlet known as 'Porthorion'. From here, the track steepens somewhat as it begins to climb towards Mynydd Analog at 192m. Although steep in places, you do not actually run all the way to its summit. Instead, the path follows the 110m contour (approx.). At GR 150275 the angle eases and a fast descent begins towards the picturesque 'Ogof Goch' and 'Porth Llanllawen' at **GR 146264**.

The stunning view towards 'Ogof Goch' and 'Porth Llanllawen' with Mynydd Mawr in the far distance.

2. From here, follow the steeply ascending grassy path still running in a Southwesterly direction. At **GR 140262** the path narrows in an elevated and exposed position.

Run carefully along this section, passing under some rocky outcrops high up on your left. Just past these, a vague line/path allows one to scramble up steep tussocks and rocks to arrive at the top of 'Mynydd Mawr' at 150m and its car park/viewpoint at **GR 140259**. There are excellent views across the sea (Bardsey Sound) towards Bardsey Island. At the summit of Mynydd Mawr locate a grassy track that provides a fast descent towards the car park at **GR 143257**.

3. A Short section of tarmac leads one to a caravan site. A path runs alongside the right-hand edge of the site. An 'optional' ascent can be made here of 'Mynydd Gwyddel' (99m) by taking the broad grassy track to its rounded top at **GR 142252**.

Back at the caravan site, run the gently descending path towards the cliff edge at **GR 144250** and marked as Porth Felen. Continue South-east along the narrow path which heads towards the impressive rocky cove known as 'Parwyd' (**GR 154244**). From here, run along the ascending 'perimeter fence' towards the point known as ' Mynydd Bychestyn' at **GR 153246**. There is a National Trust 'honesty collection box' here!

Julia Kelly pushing hard up the steep slope of the lower section of Mynydd Mawr.

4. Head East now across fields towards a farm at **GR 158246**. During wet weather, the field here can become quite muddy. From the farmhouse, run along the minor track/lane to a sharp left turn at **GR 158251**. A signed footpath on the right directs one to 'Porth Cloch'. Take this path, crossing several fields towards the edge of the sea cliffs. The path improves here and now heads in a Northerly direction to 'Porth Meudy' and its boat-launching slipway. This is accessed via a steeply descending, hillside staircase. Now follow the ascending staircase on the opposite side of Porth Meudy (bit a thigh 'pump' here!) to arrive at a good path that leads one towards the lovely coastal village of Aberdaron. At Aberdaron, there are two options available:

1/. Descend the minor road into Aberdaron but take the first left at

GR 172265, signposted 'Whistling Sands/ Porthorion'. This quiet lane can be followed for the next couple of miles, passing the 'lookout' tower at Mynydd Carreg (**GR 164292**). From here, your parked car is only a ¼ mile away.

2/. Descend fully in to Aberdaron (Spar Shop refreshments during normal opening hours!) and take the B4413 for a short distance out of the village, picking up the coastal path as it follows the 'Afon Daron' in North-easterly direction. At **GR 182268**, turn left and follow the path across pasture land, crossing the B4413 again at **GR 179274**. The path now continues to cross fields, meeting a cross-roads at **GR 175282**. It now takes the minor road Northwards for a short distance. At **GR 176287**, the path heads due West across more fields. Eventually,the route emerges at the minor road below Mynydd Carreg at **GR 166291**.

Whichever way you choose to complete this trail run, take a few moments afterwards to reflect on the fact that you have just completed one of the best trail runs in this beautiful, unspoilt corner of North Wales. Spread the word!

Parys Mountain Circuit

ROUTE 13

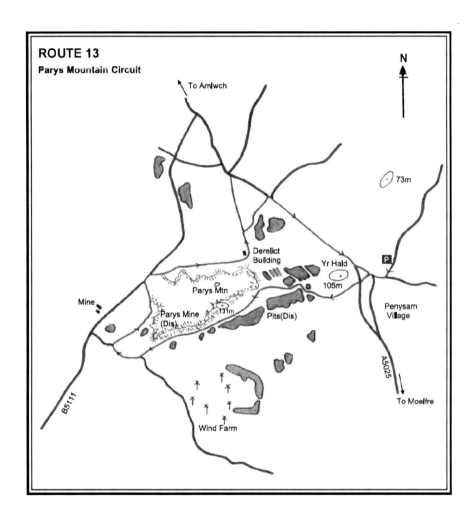

ROUTE 13

Parys Mountain Circuit

N

To Amlwch

73m

Derelict Building

Yr Hald

P

Parys Mtn

105m

Mine

Parys Mine (Dis)

131m

Pits(Dis)

Penysarn Village

B5111

A5025

To Moelfre

Wind Farm

120

ROUTE 13: PARYS MOUNTAIN CIRCUIT

DISTANCE: 4.75 Miles
ASCENT: Min. 85 metres @ start. Max.130 metres.
TERRAIN: Imagine what the planet Mars might look like! Well, this is probably the nearest you will get to it, certainly in the UK. Although not the longest route, this amazing trail run passes through what was, in the 18th and 19th Centuries, the largest and most productive copper mine in the world, supplying its valuable metal to sheath the wooden hulls of ships and manufacture canons. Now all that remains is a disused, alien world of ochre and red coloured rock with high cliffs and piles of scree, extracted from a gigantic opencast mine. It's a bit like James Bond 007 meets War of the Worlds! It is a truly fascinating place.

This route is run entirely on public footpaths and quarry tracks with some short tarmac sections on roads at the start and finish. Some of the path sections at the beginning are becoming a touch overgrown with low, calf-height gorse bushes! Don't wear ankle socks! The distant views of the town of Amlwch and the Anglesey coastline are superb.
TIME: 50mins - 1hr.15mins approx.(depending on stops).
START: Penysarn Village free car park at **GR 462906**
O.S MAP: 1:25,000 Anglesey Coast Sheet O.S. 263
GRADIENT: Gentle gradients throughout.
ACCESS: No known access problems. However, please be aware that you enter this area of mine workings at 'your own risk' and several disclaimer signs remind visitors of this.

Grid References

462906 Free car park in Penysarn Village
460906 Left turn into 'Lon Tyddyn Waen'
454904 Stone bridge between two small lakes
438897 Junction between quarry track and minor road
435898 Right turn signposted 'Bryn Pary's Cottage'
438906 B5111
447909 Derelict mine building
447911 Right turn on to tarmac road
450915 A5025
459908 Turn in to Penysarn Village

FGS Grading: Grading is T2 [D0, N1, T0, R1, H0]

Distance	0	Up to 6 miles
Navigation	1	Basic navigation skills needed
Terrain	0	75%+ on graded track or path
Remoteness	1	Countryside in fairly close proximity to habitation – at least 80% of the route within 2 miles
Height	0	Less than 100 ft per mile

Route Description :

1. From the main A5025 road towards Amlwch take a right turn into the village of Penysarn. Locate the free car park at the northern end of the village and park here. Turn right out of the car park and run through the village in a westerly direction. After a short distance you will reach a no through road on the left, named Lon Tyddyn Waen (**GR 460906**). Take this and follow it under the A5025 to a gate, which gives access to a footpath and open country. This section of track is overgrown in places and can get muddy in wet weather. Follow this through several more gates until it reaches open grassland and the quarry's 'settling beds', now a series of picturesque, small lakes.

The marked footpath allows one to run across a small stone bridge separating two small lakes (**GR 454904**). Turn right after the bridge and remain on the slightly rising path (low gorse bushes here!) as it passes another small lake. The path improves somewhat here and increases in size, turning

into a long straight quarry road heading in a south-easterly direction.

Passing the second small lake after the stone bridge. Photos: Julia Kelly

Ascending the country lane towards Bryn Pary's cottage.

2. Huge red and brown scree slopes of copper ore pour down the hillside on your right at this point. A taster for what is to come in a little while! After a mile or so an ascending tarmac country lane is reached (**GR 438897**). Follow this uphill, passing some residential houses. At **GR 435898** a track, sign-posted 'Bryn Pary's Cottage' is met on the right. Take this and run along the narrow path that now gives access to the top of the mine workings.

The views from here become increasingly spectacular as one approaches the quarry 'rim'. A purpose-built 'belvedere' for visitors gives the best view of the vast copper

Running towards the rim of the main quarry with the old Summit Windmill Tower on the skyline. Photo: Julia Kelly.

mine workings that stretch out before you. It really is "Wow! & Oooohhh!" stuff.

The spectacular view from the ''belvedere' showing the copper mine in all its colours ! Photo: Jim Kelly

3. From the viewpoint, continue north until you reach the B5111 (**GR 438906**). A very short section on this allows you to connect with the continuation footpath that rises gradually in an easterly direction. A round tower on top of the hill marks the point where the path begins to descend towards a large, ruined mine building at **GR 447909**.

4. Upon reaching the ruin, take a left and head north along a stony track. After a short distance a crossroads is met at **GR 447911**. Turn right here onto the tarmac road and head towards the A5025. Cross this road and turn right, running along the pavement back towards Penysarn Village, which lies approximately a mile away.

ROUTE 14

Beddgelert Forest Trail

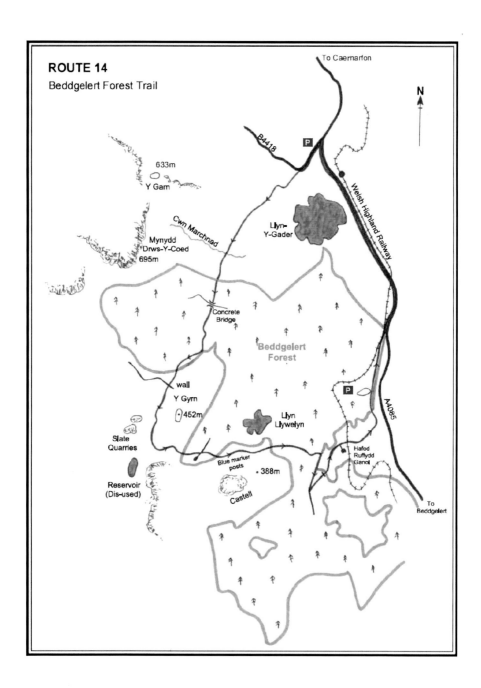

ROUTE 14
Beddgelert Forest Trail

ROUTE 14: BEDDGELERT FOREST TRAIL

DISTANCE: 6.5 Miles
ASCENT: Min. 145 metres. Max. 424 metres.
TERRAIN: This delightful route is 'sandwiched' between the Snowdon Massif to the east and the Nantlle Ridge to the west. It provides a scenic trail run between these two major land forms. Although it is run entirely on public footpaths, the nature of those narrow paths is quite challenging. There are surface stones and rocks throughout interspersed with sections of tree roots, and boggy tussock grass. Running on them requires a good level of concentration. Much of the rock is slate or 'shale' in nature so it can become a touch on the slippery side, especially during damp or wet weather. During the Autumn and winter months, some of the ground away from the forestry tracks can become quite wet and boggy. Anticipate wet feet so, pack some dry socks and a towel for afterwards!

However, the rewards are well worth the effort. There is a real feel of remoteness about it with a fine, balanced mix between woodland and 'open' mountain terrain.
TIME: 1 Hour 30 mins. Approx. depending on the conditions under foot.
START: Park on the B4418, at lay-by on the right just above Rhyd-Ddu Village (GR 568528).
O.S MAP: 1:25,000 Sheet North Wales OL17.
GRADIENT: Steady gradients in both ascent and descent. Some sections of steep rocky steps.
ACCESS: No known access restrictions. There are several gates to pass through. Please ensure these are closed after you to prevent livestock straying.

Grid References

568528 Parking at Rhyd-Ddu.
558517 Stream crossing at Cwm Marchnad
558515 Entry point into Beddgelert Forest
552504 gate in drystone wall
550499 Path to Bwlch cwm-trwsgi
558496 Start of 'boggy' path
563497 Re-entry to Beddgelert Forest
572497 Railway crossing
574503 Forestry Commission car park
576509 A4085 road

127

FGS Grading: Grading is T7 [D1, N2, T1, R2, H1]

Distance	1	6 – 12 miles
Navigation	2	Competent navigation skills needed
Terrain	1	50 – 75% on graded track or path 25 – 50% off track.
Remoteness	2	Countryside not in close proximity to habitation – less than 20% of the route within 2 miles
Height	1	Over 100 ft per mile

Route Description :

1. From the lay-by parking above Rhyd-Ddu, run along the B4418 for a short distance to a sharp right hand bend. At the bend a gate on the left allows access to a good path extending over rough pasture towards Y Garn (633m) and the Nantlle Ridge. Continue steadily upwards along a narrow, stony path, which is boggy in a couple of sections. However, some deft footwork over the tussocks and reeds allows one to avoid the worst bits. A small stream cascades down the hillside at Cwm Marchnad (**GR 558517**) and acts as a point of reference.

Jim Kelly running along the initial section, just before entering Beddgelert Forest. Photo: Julia Kelly

2. The path now 'flattens' somewhat and, after a short distance, the edge of Beddgelert Forest is met (**GR 558515**). Proceed along the often-boggy footpath, as it descends gently to emerge at a forestry track and a small concrete bridge over a stream. Follow the forestry road gently uphill until a broken, rocky path is reached, rising through trees on the left. During wet spells, this path carries a small stream. Although not shown on the O.S. Map, there is an extensive area of felled trees over to your right.

Eventually, the angle begins to descend towards the remains of some old slate quarries, accessed via a gate in a dry stone wall at **GR 552504**. Take care running on the smooth slate surface rocks and boulders, especially if they are wet or damp. Under these conditions, slate has little friction.

Descending the steep slate path through the quarries. Photo: Julia Kelly.

3. Head towards the distant reservoir (disused) that can be seen lower down the valley. However, before this at **GR 550499**, a small, broken path extends leftwards up and over more rocks and large boulders around the lower slopes of 'Y Gryn' (452m) and marked as, Bwlch Cwm-trwsgi.

After a short distance, a wet, marshy area is met and avoided by running alongside a high stone wall. Immediately after this, the forest is re-entered and the continuation path emerges at a wide forestry track with a dead-end to the right. Therefore, your only option is to turn left. After approximately 50 metres the 'continuation' footpath is way marked to your right. Take care here as this section is prone to being wet and slippery over exposed tree roots and rocks. This rising path eventually emerges onto another 'open', marshy area with some rocky outcrops (**GR 558496**). The footpath 'line' here is quite indistinct and has been marked by a series of short blue wooden stakes. However, be prepared for wet feet crossing this area, in all but the driest of weather.

4. At **GR 563497**, Beddgelert Forest is entered yet again, via a low stile. As before, take care on this section as it descends some steep, slippery terrain with many exposed tree roots and surface stones.

After a stony descent, the sanctuary of a wide forestry road is met. Follow this road south for a couple of minutes until another obvious, descending track is reached on the left. Run down this, passing a locked, yellow and black painted, metal barrier gate.

Approaching the metal barrier gate. Photo: Julia Kelly.

5. At the next junction, turn right and run this good, descending road passing, the dwelling, 'Hafod Ruffydd Ganol' which is on your right hand side. At **GR 572497**, cross the narrow gauge, Welsh Highland Railway line and proceed down the track that connects with the footpath running parallel to the 'Afon Colwyn' and on to the Forestry Commission car park at **GR 574503**.

6. At **GR 576509**, the main A4085 between Caernarfon and Beddgelert is reached. Turn left and run along this northwards back to Rhyd-Ddu. There are superb views of Snowdon (1085m) and Yr Aran (747m) over to your right.

Upon reaching Rhyd-Ddu, run past the public house (maybe pay a visit later?!) and, at the phone box, turn sharp right and follow the B4418 back to your waiting car.

ROUTE 15

Penmachno North Forest Circuit

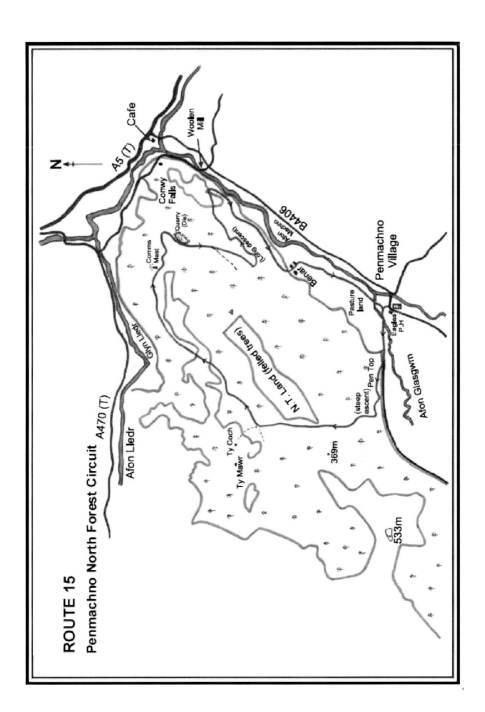

ROUTE 15
Penmachno North Forest Circuit

N

A5 (T)
Cafe
Woolen Mill
Conwy Falls
B4406
Afon Machno
Quarry (Dis)
Comms Mast
(Long descent)
Benar
Penmachno Village
Pasture land
N.T. Land (felled trees)
Eagles P.H.
Pen Top
(steep ascent)
Afon Glasgwm
Ty Coch
Ty Mawr
369m
533m
Afon Lledr
Gwyn Lledr
A470 (T)

ROUTE 15: PENMACHNO NORTH FOREST CIRCUIT

DISTANCE: 7 ¼ Miles
ASCENT: Min. 150 metres @ start. Max. 340 metres.
TERRAIN: : Penmachno is famed for annually hosting two stages of the famous Lombard/Network Q World Rally Championships back in the 1980's and 1990's. Although rallying still takes place here (Cambrian Rally Wales), long gone are the days of hearing the awesome, turbo-popping Group B cars of Colin McRae (RIP), Malcolm Wilson and Didier Auriol, hurtling past at over 100mph, only two foot away from suicidal rally spectators!

Today, Penmachno's forest trails and tracks are usually only disturbed by the squeaking brakes of mountain bikers and the crunching of gravel under trail runner's feet! Some would argue this is a 'tad' more environmentally acceptable. In terms of excitement? Well, you make your own judgement as far as that one is concerned…(he says with muffled cough!)

A steep uphill section of tarmac at the beginning gives way to typically wide, gravel-surfaced, undulating, fast forestry trails on which to run. Open, valley pasture land, during the later stages of the route, gives a fine end to this great run.
TIME: : 1 Hour 30-45 mins. approx.
START: : Park in the delightful village of Penmachno, GR 790505 (2 miles from the A5(T) road from Betws y Coed, taking the B4406) after crossing the bridge over the 'Afon Machno'. There are several places to park nearby to the excellent 'Eagles' Public House. Make sure you do not obstruct anyone's access or driveway. The village roads are very narrow. Please be sensitive to this.
O.S MAP: 1:25,000 Sheet North Wales OL18.
GRADIENT: An initial steep, uphill section is followed by more gentle, easy-angled forestry tracks and roads, both in ascent and descent. A final horizontal stage across grass fields provides a satisfying end to this trail run.
ACCESS: No known access issues. The 'area' welcomes outdoor enthusiasts. However, please make sure all countryside signs are obeyed and be aware that cyclists, walkers and Forestry Commission machinery frequently use and operate in this area.

Grid References

790505 Starting point – Penmachno Village
776523 Forestry track on the right
782527 Area of open fields
788534 Track forks
794535 Communications mast
795523 Sharp left turn
805528 Woolen Mill
794518 'Benar Cottages'

FGS Grading: Grading is T5 [D1, N1, T0, R2, H1]

Distance	1	6 -12 miles
Navigation	1	Basic navigation skills needed
Terrain	0	75% + on graded track or path
Remoteness	2	Countryside not in close proximity to habitation – less than 20% of the route within 2 miles.
Height	1	Over 100 ft per mile

Route Description :

1. Begin in Penmachno Village. At The Eagles Public House, take the minor road sign-posted 'Ty Mawr'/ 'Ty Goch' (National Trust). This narrow lane splits after half a mile or so. Take the right hand fork to 'Ty Mawr'. This tarmac lane rises steeply for another good half mile, passing 'Pen Top' and a parking lay-by a little further on. This section is a popular start/ finish point for mountain bikers so expect cars and vans parked up here.

As one reaches the 320 – 330m contour, the road begins to flatten, passing an open, extensive, cleared area of trees fenced off and under N. T. ownership.

Jim Kelly descending towards the junction at GR 776523.
Photo: Julia Kelly.

2. The tarmac lane now descends. Run down this as far as GR 776523 where a good forestry road appears on the right hand side. Take this track as it descends gently, passing an area of open fields and good views to your left at GR 782527.

Continue running, keeping to the right hand track to where it forks at GR 788534. The track now begins to ascend once again, passing a very obvious communications mast at GR 794535. The track continues to rise to the 300m contour where it passes a disused quarry on the left and on to another obvious fork. Take the left-hand continuation as it now descends in a southerly direction to a sharp left turn at GR 795523, where it heads Northeast but, still descending. Before the

Running past the area of open country side before the track forks to the right. Photo: Julia Kelly.

'Woolen Mill' at GR 805528, the track takes another sharp turn – this time to the right.

By now, you have descended almost to the valley floor where you will see glimpses of the Afon Machno through the trees.

3. Proceed along the wide forestry track as it rises ever so slightly towards a group of cottages named 'Benar' (GR 794518). At Benar follow the yellow footpath 'arrows' over a stile and down through a field to the side of the cottages.

Just after the 300m contour at the point where the track splits left. Photo: Julia Kelly.

The path now continues across grass fields in a South-westerly direction, passing over another stile. Run towards some disused farm cottages where an access road leads straight back in to Penmachno Village

Almost finished ! Jim Kelly approaching Benar Cottages before crossing
the fields that make up the Afon Machno Valley. The pub is all but
10 minutes away! . Photo: Julia Kelly.

emerging, very conveniently, at The Eagles Public House! Go on, treat
yourself! "Mine's a pint – what are you having?"

ROUTE "TICK" LIST					
ROUTE NO.	√	Date / Time Achieved	Weather Conditions	Partner(s) / Group	Remarks
1					
2					
3					
4					
5					
6					
7					
8					
9					
10					
11					
12					

ROUTE "TICK" LIST

ROUTE NO.	√	Date / Time Achieved	Weather Conditions	Partner(s) / Group	Remarks
13					
14					
15					
Notes					

Jim Kelly: Jim Kelly was born in London in 1963. He first entered outdoor sports whilst at school in the late 1970's and early 80's. Climbing became his main passion with early ascents of Alpine Peaks such as Mont Blanc and Monte Rosa/ Dufourspitze between 1982 and 1983. Thereafter, Jim went on to instruct climbing and caving at several outdoor centres in England and Wales. In 1988 he moved to Sheffield in order to undertake a degree in Sports and Recreation Management. It also allowed him plenty of time to climb in the Peak District! More recently, Jim moved to North Wales where mountain running has become a new 'obsession' with him. It also happens to be where he met Julia, his wife. In his first 18 months of running Jim has completed both the arduous Snowdonia Marathon (his first ever marathon attempt!) in 03:44:05 and went on to complete the International Snowdon Run in a very respectable 01:35:07. Although Jim now works in retailing, guide book writing and feature writing for running and climbing magazines is increasingly absorbing more and more of his spare time. With several other titles in the pipeline, the future looks set to become a whole lot busier for him!

Julia Kelly: Julia Kelly was born in Indonesia in 1967 where she trained as a merchandising manager for many big-name designer fashion houses. She came over to the UK in 2007 where she met and married Jim. Julia has keen interest in rock climbing, mountain scrambling, photography and design. Her knowledge of information technology has been invaluable in the production of this guide. Most recently Julia & Jim have established "Run to the Hills (North Wales)" guided off-road running services for beginners and experienced runners alike.

Trailguides Limited and the Run Off-Road Series

Trailguides is a small independent publisher specialising in books for the outdoor enthusiast. Run Off-Road is the name adopted by Trailguides for it's publications aimed at the fell, hill, trail and mountain runner. This series of books is designed to promote the sport of off-road running in all it's many forms and to encourage the participants to improve and develop their abilities and skills in order to further increase their enjoyment of the sport.

Our range of coaching guides for the fell, trail and mountain runner have received acclaim and favourable reviews from all of the relevant UK governing bodies within the sport, the Fell Runners Association, the Scottish Hill Runners Association, the Trail Runners Association and the Welsh Fell Runners Association plus the Irish Mountain Runners Association. Written by qualified coaches who specialise in off-road running these books often receive comments that they are unique in their concept and, indeed, have even been called that in one issue of The Fellrunner magazine. Our guiding principle is that our books "don't just tell you what to do but they also tell you HOW to do it".

This concept has been recognised by sales not only in the UK but across the world. Books have been sold to Australia, Canada, El Salvador, Finland, France, Germany, Ireland, Italy, Netherlands, New Zealand, Norway, Slovakia, Slovenia, South Africa, Spain, Sweden, Switzerland and the US. The expertise and popularity of our books is judged by the number of runners who buy one and who then come back to purchase others within the series.

This is an evolving series of books that is constantly expanding and now with this publication, The Trail Runner's Guide to North Wales, the second volume in our new range of guidebooks written specifically for the runner, continues this expansion. Designed to both encourage runners to venture away from the dreaded tarmac and to also push their capabilities just a little bit, this series will develop into a range of guides that will cover the countryside throughout the country ranging from the mountain tops of Snowdonia to the rolling hills of the South Downs and the flat lands of Norfolk. This is a series of books that will appeal to all of the fell, mountain and trail runners out there.

See our website at www.trailguides.co.uk and subscribe to our newsletter for regular updates on our range of publications.

At the time of writing the titles in the series include:

An Introduction to Trail and Fell Running
Downhill Techniques for Off-Road Runners
Uphill Techniques for Off-road Runners
Terrain Training for Off-road Runners
Mountain Marathon Preparation
Navigation for Off-Road Runners
Long and Ultra Distance Off-Road Running
The Mountain Marathon Book

Coming soon
The Trail Running Book

Guide books:

A Mountain Runner's Guide to Snowdonia
A Trail Runner's Guide to North Wales

Coming soon
A Trail & Fell Runner's Guide to the Lake District: South Eastern Area.

Disclaimer

The information contained in these pages and the route descriptions is provided in good faith, but no warranty is made for its accuracy. The contents are, at the time of writing and to the best of our knowledge, up-to-date and correct. However, the world is a changing environment and what is correct one day may not be so the next. Care should always be taken when following these route descriptions just as it should when following maps or waymarkers of any kind..

No guarantee whatsoever is provided by the author and/or Trailguides Limited and no liability is accepted for any loss, damage or injury of any kind resulting from the use of this book, nor as a result of any defect or inaccuracy in it.

As with all outdoor activities, you and you alone are responsible for your safety and well being.

Trail running is one of the fastest developing areas of physical fitness and the countryside of North Wales is one of the most scenic parts of the UK in which to practice it. With a rugged coastline, lush countryside, deep, sylvan forests and all set against the backdrop of the high mountains of Snowdonia, this part of Wales is a joy upon which to plant the trainer.

In a series of fifteen runs, join the authors as they set foot to trail on some of the most exhilarating running routes within the UK. Beach, coast, field, forest and hill, to the runner who wants to get away from the mundane of pounding the tarmac these are some of the most stirring words in the English language. If you've never tried trail running then let this book guide you to some of the most memorable running experiences around. If you are a veteran of the trail running scene then, in the two writers, you've got expert guidance to routes that you simply must put foot to.

To the runner, running may be a necessity but there are some runs you just owe it to yourself to experience...

TRAIL GUIDES
publications

35 Carmel Road South
Darlington, County Durham
DL3 8DQ
www.trailguides.co.uk

ISBN 978-1-905444-50-2

£15.99